These Boys Are Killing Me

Travels and Travails With Sons Who Take Risks

TERRY BAKER MULLIGAN

These Boys Are Killing Me
Travels and Travails With Sons Who Take Risks
Terry Baker Mulligan
Impulse Press

Published by Impulse Press, St. Louis, MO
Copyright ©2019 Terry Baker Mulligan
All rights reserved.

Cover and Interior design: Davis Creative, DavisCreative.com

Library of Congress Cataloging-in-Publication Data

Library of Congress Control Number: 2019904091

Terry Baker Mulligan

These Boys Are Killing Me: Travels and Travails With Sons Who Take Risks

ISBN: 978-0-9846929-5-8 (paperback)
       978-0-9846929-6-5 (case laminate)

Library of Congress subject headings:

1. TRV002000 TRAVEL / Africa / General 2. SOC042000 SOCIAL SCIENCE / Developing & Emerging Countries 3. BIO023000 BIOGRAPHY & AUTOBIOGRAPHY / Adventurers & Explorers

2019

Dedication

To Brennan and Colin

Table of Contents

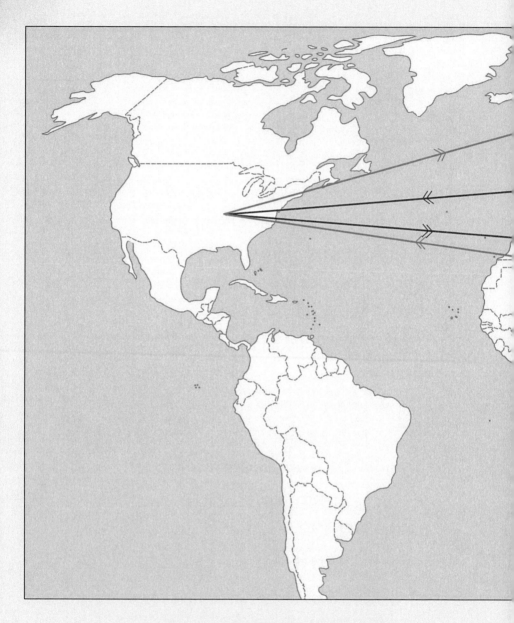

Brennan: ———
Egypt, Israel, Jordan, Syria, Lebanon,
Iraq, Italy—then home

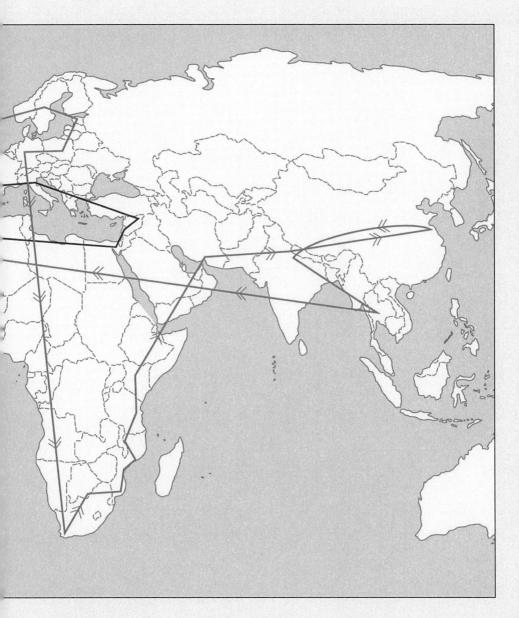

Colin:

Holland, Copenhagen, Sweden, Estonia, Latvia, Lithuania, Poland, Germany, Austria, Italy, Belgium, South Africa, Swaziland, Mozambique, Malawi, Tanzania, Kenya, UAE, Oman, Iran, China, Tibet, Nepal, Thailand, Laos—then home

Foreword

My sons swam the deep waters on three continents, and backpacked up the highest mountains. Over a period of eighteen months they were embraced by people from multiple cultures, ethnicities, religions, and ways of life. Sometimes I admonished them for risky behavior, but then I'd be elated to hear when families welcomed them into their homes, or Muslims embraced them inside their mosques. Friends in seventeen countries enjoined them to dance and carry on—along with a beer, or two, or three—in night clubs, at beach parties and street festivals. So, to protect some privacies, I changed several names and locations, or masked identities. Also, due to space and length considerations, I shortened or edited many emails.

When I received a message calling for clarification, I'd simply ask for an explanation. A good example was Colin writing about wearing sandals at Mount Everest base camp because his feet were sore and blistered. Over the years, I'd forgotten many details from my first reading of their emails—which frankly, I mostly speed-read for assurance that they were safe, rather than astonishment at their adventures. So, naturally I questioned why he'd be wearing sandals in what I assumed was cold and snowy terrain. Colin explained and I clarified the scenario after relaying his experience.

These pages tell stories of two young men who seek their place in the universe and in the world. You'd have to ask them if they found all they were looking for. What I do know is that they discovered a world community and, because they were willing to share it, I will forever remain grateful.

"Then, one day when you least expect it, the great adventure finds you."

–Ian McGregor:

abundance. Instead of rebuilding, re-settling and re-occupy
town, it was being used to further ~~was~~ an agenda in one
se pointless conflicts I was writing about. In saying this,
ly mean to take sides—just to emphasize my view that war and
current state of war that exists in the region is patently stupi
wasteful. It represents the complete failure and breakdown
civilized methods of discourse and dispute resolution. ~~War~~ A
think about it, war is the best definition or synonym for th
d "shameful" that I can think of.

These were my thoughts as we toured the town of Quneitra
n our guide — a Syrian in plainclothes who didn't say much
guide's english wasn't too good, but his ~~target~~ real reas
being there was to ensure that we didn't wander int
y mined areas or otherwise cause a disturbance.
ne of the things we missed out on was the yelling
tches that are said to occur between civilians on both
des of the divide. The Let's Go book indicates:

"On some days, especially Fridays, you can see families
yelling at each other by megaphone between the Golan
and the Syrian UN border (only 2km), adding a
human face to a conflict plaguing the Middle East."

are were troops all around — armed ~~civilians~~ Syrian police an
d (the majority) UN troops stationed in fortifications a
over as well. Yet in spite of all that there were also
ilians in small towns too. In the distance on the Israe
de there were fields that looked well-irrigated with
ps growing ~~all~~ ~~over~~ throughout. If there wasn't essent
forced peace ~~that~~ was held in place by the UN, the area would
~~ultimate~~ simply be a bombed-out warzone wasteland.

the visit to Quneitra happened on our last day in Damascus. I woke
up early the next day so I could get a tear in my sandal repaired
at a nearby shop before we headed to the bus station. Next stop
Beirut.

7/3

I don't know ~~whether you're caused~~ what causes one to automatically
perceive differences in terrain when traveling from one country to another.
So far on this trip, I've noticed pronounced differences between the
landscapes of the 4 countries I've visited. I am undecided as to
whether or not this is caused by real ~~or~~ or perceived differences
our entrance into Lebanon, I think, ~~was caused by~~ came as
close to as any place due to presenting us with an entirely
different landscape. The first thing you notice is that you're no
longer in the desert and the humidity you know so well

Part One

St. Louis is back ~~~~ through the country to
Beirut you pass mountains that are high enough to have ski
resorts that operate during the winter. Coming into Beirut, I
witnessed ~~my~~ the first significant cloud formations I had seen
almost 3 months — still no rain though.
At some point I think I should cover or discuss an event
raised my guard when I met locals these days. When I was in
Dahab I got an e-mail message from Badwy Said in Luxor.
the time since I left Luxor, I had been exchanging a few
messages with him — pleasantries generally. After about
such messages I got one from him that said, basically
at the family ~~is~~ was very sad because their father
had taken ill. He said that his father was in the ICU
that the care that was being provided at the hospital
was very expensive. The favor that he asked of me was
deposit $1000 in an Egyptian bank of my choice so
could get access to it for his father's care.

Chapter 1

Doing This Thing

The safe place that is home is always a tempting option.

It was Sunday, April 15, 2001. Beyoncé was still with Destiny's Child, George W. was our new president and, no one had ever heard of Twitter or Instagram. Late that morning, I was at Lambert St. Louis Airport, feeling less than joyous, but trying to set the right tone as we said goodbye to our older son, Brennan. For such an eventful trip, this was a pretty low key departure. At dinner the previous night, we'd showered Brennan with goodbyes and good lucks. Mike and the boys cracked jokes, most of them with me as the butt, as usually happened when our family foursome got together.

"Mom, are you going to worry yourself to death, now that you can't pick up the phone to call one of Brennan's friends—or the police," Colin stressed, rolling his eyes—"like you used to, when you couldn't find one of us for a few hours? In the Middle East, he'll be off the grid."

"Well, that time you were eight, and disappeared, I did call the police because you'd never gone missing for so long without calling me. And, you may remember, as you two got older, and apparently much less wise, it was usually the police calling here! But, to answer your question, now I'll have to call the embassy."

"Jesus," Colin said, ignoring my reference to the hellish days and nights they caused over the years, "you're not serious, I hope?"

"I am, and worrying about my kids is a mother's job. Someone has to worry since your father doesn't sweat a thing. He even sleeps through the phone if it rings at two, three, or four in the morning, which it unfortunately did, too many times when you two began acting like rules and laws didn't apply to you."

"Pricks," Mike, my husband interjected in typical Dad shorthand, "is what they were acting like."

By 11 a.m. the next day, the laughs and remember-whens had ended and I watched Brennan board a TWA flight to Chicago where, later that evening, he would transfer to a Swiss Air DC-10 bound for Zürich. The last leg of his 24 hour odyssey would be to Cairo, Egypt, his final destination. Before all hell broke loose a few months later on September 11th, you could literally watch your kid saunter down a jetway, boarding pass in hand, and disappear for an indeterminate length of time, without a plan, or a place to live, and only $200 in his pocket. Insufficient funds was just one of several troubling factors. I didn't understand Brennan's timing—good job, his first solo apartment—or purpose of this trip, which felt like running away. From what, I didn't know.

In the process of leaving, he'd successfully unencumbered himself of life's details: housing (left when the lease ended on his furnished apartment), employment (quit), and stuff (dumped what he'd scavenged from our house, back at our house). There were many, but the biggest red flag was when he said he wasn't sure if he'd be back in time for one of his best friend's weddings, still seven months away.

Often, young travelers who plan an exotic, indefinite adventure, do it right out of college, not when they're 26, beginning to forsake hell-raising and starting to get their act together with career-building, a relationship, or graduate school: three things Brennan had no interest in.

In the 1990s, when Brennan got out of college, the economy soared, a tech boom was created, and thousands of new technical jobs were filled by hotshot college grads who jumped right into the new thing called the World Wide Web. At Brennan's university, a kid named Ming started teaching computer coding languages to Brennan and some other friends on Saturday mornings, because the university's curriculum hadn't yet caught up with brainiacs like Ming.

Brennan, one of these early generation computer engineers, switched jobs about as often as the seasons changed—while still in college. He and his fellow techies knew more than managers and CEO's who were desperate to "get online." Bosses let him set up their systems, wire them, troubleshoot, and do whatever was needed. At one point in the middle of his last semester, Brennan called to say, "Mom, college is getting in the way of my job." He thought this state of nirvana would last forever. It wasn't until his diploma arrived, three months after graduation, that I finally believed he'd fully matriculated.

———

One night, at a dinner party, I sat next to a psychologist and we ended up talking about the behavior of young men. Until then, I'd never paid much attention to the science of adolescent brain development. Then, a few days later, on April 18, 2017, the New York Times ran an article, by Tim Requarth titled "A Court Calls on Science." Requarth reported on scientific studies affirming that human self-control and risk-taking is governed by the dorsolateral prefrontal cortex section of the brain. This area often doesn't finish developing until a person is between 18-20 years-old. In many, if not most instances, the prefrontal cortex is not fully developed until an individual is in his mid-twenties, to nearly thirty years-old, or beyond. These findings have given rise to "young adult courts" that work with adolescents and young people. Their intent is to keep kids out of adult prisons, giving them a chance to reform, but it's also an opportunity for young offenders to grow and mature.

Frequently, people say it takes boys longer to mature. I couldn't agree more, although girls too, display unacceptable behaviors. However, over the years, I saw my share of destructive behavior, mostly male, in schools where I worked. It happened to a tenth grader when I first taught high school. He was with another boy in downtown St. Louis, at the Clarion Hotel. While robbing the gift shop, the other kid shot and killed the cashier. Sometimes I still think of our student, who was in my friend, Phyllis Bernstein's class. She described him as respectful, well mannered; a good kid. But, in the eyes of the law, being a good kid didn't count for much. He was complicit in the murder of an innocent woman.

I closely followed that case because Mr. Dwyer, my next-door neighbor, was the lead detective. There were no young adult courts then. That skinny, quiet, brown-skinned young man, with a close-cropped haircut and a grief-stricken mother, was going to the big house with hardened criminals. He didn't stand a chance.

On many occasions, I saw a lack of maturity, self-control and a pattern of poor decision-making by my sons. No one ever died, but they could have. Raising them is a challenge, and boys have their own ways of messing with your head. Sometimes you want to strangle them, or throw things at their head, like a telephone, which I once did. I can't recall what made me so angry, but I remember that I wasn't so out of control as to not miss on purpose.

As parents, we must keep guiding our children, and loving them, even on days we don't like them very much. I still thank God for His large and small mercies, because I don't believe we can do it without Him. Was it God who prevented anyone from getting hurt or killed on that hot August night when Brennan's still open prefrontal cortex prevented him from having the good sense God gave him to not drive, after drinking too much on his 21st birthday? And, why didn't the cop shoot, rather than say, "You don't know how close I came to shooting…," when we met him in juvenile court, a few weeks after he caught 16 year-old Colin and his friends shooting at cars with a paint pellet gun that looked just like an assault rifle?

More recently, a 21 year-old University of Virginia student, Otto Warmbier—reportedly off-the-chart smart, the salutatorian of his high school class—pulled what some might consider a fairly harmless college boy prank. Unfortunately, he did it in a North Korean hotel. In 2015, when Otto spotted a poster on the wall of his hotel, he single-mindedly wanted that cool souvenir so, by God, he took it.

Touring North Korea, already defined him as a risk taker, an extreme traveler, whose interests weren't limited to drinking rum punch in Jamaica, or skiing Vail. He relished the new and daring; felt energized by the unknown, but didn't consider the consequences—fifteen years in prison, with hard labor, and tragically, death. Otto was like many adventurous young men. He was like my sons.

Cairo
From: Brennan M Mulligan
To: Theresa Mulligan
Date: April 16 2001
Subject: All okay

Hi Mom and Dad,
I arrived in Cairo at sundown. From the
airplane, the city's buildings were the
same color as desert sand in the distance.
Most noticeable were the apartment
buildings that looked like cement beehives
stacked on top of one another. When I
finally got to bed, I was surrounded by
minarets blaring the sunset call to prayer
and serenaded by a chorus of car horns.
I'd leaped into a different world, amid new
and wondrous experiences; then I slept for
two days.

You get hustled everywhere you go. It was
a total shit show at Giza. They won't
leave you alone. Finally, I overpaid
and took the tour on camelback. I did
everything wrong, especially choosing a
cab driver/guide parked in front of the
Nile Hilton. Some good advice I later got
is to tell these guys to "imshee" (go
away). Besides the pyramids and the Sphinx,
it's amazing to see the city of Cairo come
to an abrupt end when the pyramid grounds
begin. Beyond the pyramids to the west is
a sea of sand separating Cairo from…well…
Libya.

Over the next few weeks, Brennan further described Cairo as a sprawling city of 16 million people, with abundant trash, a cacophony of cars, donkey carts, tuk tuk scooters and people yelling. He found Tahir Square, where lots of foreigners congregated, and ate dinner with two French ex-pats who work in Lebanon. Later, they drank late night coffee at a sheesha (aka, hooka lounge) that has been open 24 hours a day for the last 200 years. He said, the metro subway was efficient; but, not the buses. They just slowed down, but never fully stopped, so (able-bodied) passengers hopped off and on moving vehicles.

Brennan was awed by the ancientness of Islamic Cairo—parts of the Sayyidna al-Hussein mosque, one of the holiest sites in Egypt, were built in the 1100s. His favorite discovery was the Khan el-Khalili souq, a miles long open-air market that was established about eight centuries ago, and where he said, "You could find literally anything in the world, except maybe some car models."

"Surprisingly," he wrote, "Cairo doesn't have a cosmopolitan feel I expected, even though there are Sudanese, Moroccans, Libyans, Westerners and various other nationalities. You can feel a tug between secularists and citizens of the world-types, who drink alcohol, and live in high rise condos, etc. Some women are dressed as stylishly as those in New York or Paris. Others are covered in headscarves and veils."

From: Theresa Mulligan
To: Brennan Mulligan
Date: May 2, 2001
Subject: Cairo

Hi Brennan,

A few questions—do the cheaper hotel rooms have their own bathroom? How is the food and have you gotten sick? Your tax refund still hasn't come. I'll deposit it when it does. Dad is happy that baseball has started. I'm finishing up the semester at school and the same with your brother. He loves his job and they seem to like him, especially the boys, since young teachers are rare out there. The other day, he went ballistic when he caught a kid verbally disrespecting a maintenance guy. He took the kid aside and explained that's not how it works. I was proud of him. That was a lot better than what he told me at the beginning of the year, when the boys weren't understanding the difference between macro and micro economics.

To simplify and get their attention, he used an example of pimps and hos!!! Thank God the higher ups didn't find out, or if they did, they gave him a pass and maybe it's because they understand young men better than I do. After 26 years I'm still trying to understand what makes you two tick, like you with this trip. But I know you don't want me to rehash all that again. Just stay safe, learn something new, have fun and write.

Oh, what's the deal about boats sailing south up the Nile, rather than sailing north? I didn't understand that. Enjoy and be careful.

Love, Mom

From: Brennan Mulligan
To: Theresa Mulligan
Date: May 9, 2001
Subject: Luxor and stuff

Hi,

Yesterday, my last day in Cairo, was a
busy one. I had Shai tea (Lipton) and
chatted with Essan, a cab driver, who was
the first local I met. Later, at the train
station, while buying a first class ticket
to Luxor, ten hours away, two French
guys and I tried buying cheaper tickets,
but there seems to be a requirement for
foreigners to travel separately from
locals. I'm not sure if it's security or
an example of gouging tourists.

I'm now in Luxor, staying at the Venus
Hotel. Later, at the Mars Hotel bar I
met Jon, an American student and Phil
Porter, a 60-something retired musician
from England who often comes to Egypt and
Morocco. Phil's been around a long time
and sensed something big was going on in
the world and didn't like the climate. A
bit of a pessimist, but he's no dummy,
either.

I also went to Aswan, Kom Ombo, back to
Luxor, Hurghada, and Sharm El-Sheikh
(briefly). Jesus was it hot down there
with temperatures about 125 degrees
Fahrenheit. Cairo is hot too, but at least
the Nile was clean in the South and you
could swim in it. The Nile flows north

from the mountains in southern Africa, so
you're sailing upriver to head south.

By the way, I'm keeping a detailed journal
about some of the amazing things I've seen
and done, so someday you may get to read
that.
B

Brennan's battered journal

Chapter 2

When We Are Young

When I was raising my kids, I often forgot what I was like in my twenties. I forgot that I wasn't always a worrier, that I took chances, set off on risky travel adventures, that my mother worried about me and that she would have worried more if she knew what I did.

My long distant journey began on September 23, 1964 when I stepped on the gangway of the Queen Elizabeth, docked at Pier 90, on 46th Street along New York City's "luxury liner row." More familiarly, Pier 90 is on the Hudson River next to the old West Side Highway. Today, the Intrepid Aircraft Carrier, Air, Sea, and Space Museum occupies that space.

Since the early 20th-century, the Hudson piers have berthed famous seagoing beauties, such as the Queen Mary, the SS France and the Mauritania. That day in 1964, instead of passing the pier, a taxi deposited me at the departure area. My ultimate destination was Bregenz, Austria, a place I'd never heard of until the previous spring, when a girl in my English class said she was going to a meeting about Wagner's study program in Bregenz. "And you can earn your full year of college credit while you're there," she added.

"Is Bregenz near Vienna?" I asked.

"I don't know, but I'm sure you can find out at the meeting."

Even though I'd never traveled further than Virginia, I loved the idea of seeing the world and thought that someday I'd go to Europe. But, in 1964, I didn't know if I really wanted to go to Bregenz, or just wanted to get away from the Wagner College campus. Wagner hadn't been a good match for me and I wasn't happy there. I'd loved New Lincoln, my progressive private high school. Unlike me, many of my high school friends were wealthy and well-traveled. I didn't envy their lifestyles. Rather, through them, I saw that possibilities in life were endless. But, my Jewish friends from high school wouldn't go to Germany or Austria. If Jews weren't comfortable in the country, should I be thinking of going there?

My mother urged me to go, because she always pushed me toward worthy educational programs. Mom grew up in Depression era Harlem, where enrichment opportunities were rare for girls like her, so she wanted me to have the advantages she'd missed. With my father being a weekends-only dad who spent, rather than saved money, it was Mom and my grandmother who provided me with a solid happy childhood. Until I was twelve, we lived with Gram and our household was most definitely not a democracy. While Mom worked, Gram was my primary and autocratic caregiver. She loved me in the old Southern tradition, which included superstition, the notion that boys were Trouble, and her favorite word, "No." Despite her sometimes draconian rules, I adored her with every fiber of my being.

When I was in college, Gram was too fragile to give counsel, but she would have been as skeptical of Bregenz as I was. I pictured Nazi-types bullying Jews in the same way Southern Klansmen still terrorized black people. I asked Mom if she thought it was safe in Austria. "Of course," she countered with her usual enthusiasm. "Blacks, especially black students are beginning to travel and study in many parts of Europe. Look at Renee, your friend who's heading to the Sorbonne. And didn't you say that older girl, Linda, studied French at another university over there?"

"Yes, but Paris and other large French cities are different. They're diverse like New York. Josephine Baker and James Baldwin live there. Bregenz is a small town. No one really knows what goes on there."

I didn't tell my mother that another reason I hesitated going was that I didn't want to leave my boyfriend. But, if you asked me today who he was, I couldn't tell you.

Like me, the world was in turmoil that year. The American South was imploding with racial strife, Vietnam was disintegrating into a bloody quagmire, we were locked in a Cold War with the Soviets, and Castro had a firm grip on neighboring Cuba. I couldn't control world affairs but, destiny was in my hands; I had a return ticket. So, as I boarded the ship, I knew I could come home, if this turned out to be a mistake.

———

```
To: Mom
From: Brennan
May 11, 2001
Hey,

Luxor has been great. At a tourist
bazaar, two little kids asked what
"congratulations" meant and if I could
come into the store to write it out. I
took the bait. In response, they wanted
me to meet someone. An Arab man dressed
in a galabeya, and wearing a turban was
sitting on the floor. He stood to shake
my hand and introduced himself as Yusuf.
```

We sat drinking shai tea and a few other men joined us, including his brother, Mahmoud. There were no hard sells and as the day came to a close, Yusuf invited me to the West Bank to see his village and have dinner at his parent's home. I gladly accepted.

We took a ferry and I got my first view of the ancient city of Thebes. Among the passengers, Yusuf stuck out as much as I did. He's about 6'2," my height, and under his turban he wore dreadlocks, part of his identity as a diehard Bob Marley fan. Next, seven people crowded into a small pickup truck, with a passenger cabin mounted in the bed. We passed millennia-old, rock-carved statues and temples, and rode along the base of the desert mountain as it stretched westward into Central Egypt.

Their adobe house, situated in a settlement along a dirt road, has been in Yusuf's family for 150 years. It rains very little there; sometimes not for a year. Aside from the river and associated wells, the country is literally bone dry. We listened to Yusuf's American and western music. Later, one of his sisters brought us dinner of home-baked bread, pickled vegetables, cheese and chicken soup. I was humbled by their hospitality. I also met another sister and thanked his parents. His sisters are beautiful, but that's untouchable territory.

Brennan spent a week in Luxor with his new friends, drinking tea and beer, teaching them how to curse in English and struggling to pick up their Arabic. They also took him to a wedding reception, which he described as unlike anything he'd seen before...

The men can't hang out with the women, so single sexes eat and dance alone to the music. Yusuf cut quite a sight on the dance floor, with his galabeya and dreads, high on booze, while swaying to Bob Marley's "No Problem." We also hit a disco and spent time with a group of good looking Italian chicks.

It's been so good to have a routine, but I don't want to wear out my welcome, plus I'm itching to get to Aswan. Hope Yusuf and Mahmoud come to the States so I can put them up. I told them that I'd return in 2 to 5 days."

———

From: Brennan M Mulligan
To: Terry Mulligan
5/25/01 5:23AM

Just to let you know, I'm going to disappear for a couple of days. I met a felucca captain named "Jimi Hendrix," who will take me and 5 others on a 2-day, 2-night cruise down the Nile. We start in Luxor and end in Edfu. All food is included—a deal—the trip cost about $20. I'll take the bus back to Luxor. B

———

Diving and underwater "living room"

From: Brennan Mulligan
To: Terry Mulligan
May 30, 2001

Hi,

On the felucca cruise, a guy named Brett
told us about getting robbed, then he got
a parasitic infection. He saw a Kenyan doc
a few times for flu symptoms, high temps,
flushed skin, diarrhea. We marveled at his
determination to press on through Africa.
The cruise was great though—clear, starry
nights, a clean Nile to swim in, and at
night when we camped, one guy played his
guitar. Afterwards, I had a blast in
Hurghada; it's on the Red Sea coast and
I lived on about $10 a day. While there,
I signed up for a two day scuba diving
package and got hooked.

Now I'm in Dahab, where I'm working
on certification. Today's dive was to
a site called "the canyon." Since I'm
still in training we did not go down the
full 30 meters, but at 20 meters, I saw
thousands of small, see-through glass
fish. Their skeletons were visible, and
they swam around us and in front of the
cave entrance. When we swam towards the
entrance, they moved away in unison, like
choreographed performers. It was nothing
short of magical.

To: Brennan Mulligan
From: Terry Mulligan
June 4, 2001
Hi Brennan,

Poor Brett. I hope he spared his mother the gory
details. I'm grateful you're in a good place, mentally and
physically, and adjusting to constant fun. Will you stay
in Dahab, or continue your travels? There's still no tax
refund.

A new student has started coming into the Writing
Center. She always wants my help with her papers, so
I've gotten to know her a bit. She's a pistol and she's a
transvestite. She's very attractive and stylish, but under
her makeup, I can see traces of a beard. I know she's
taking hormones, because it was hot in the room, and
she's fanning herself and complaining to me that, she
"…needs better hormones, or more hormones, or something from that doctor."

She's got guts. One day this week, another student comes in, sees her and says: "Man, whadda you doing here? Didn't you get your ass beat the last time you were up here?" It didn't faze her a bit, but it was a reminder of what life is like for kids like her.

Sunken motorcycle and Relaxing in Dahab

```
To: Terry Mulligan
From: Brennan M
Mulligan
6/6/01
blah

Mom-

To update you on the latest, I am leaning
toward taking a job here in Dahab, at
Nesima--the dive shop in town. It doubles
as a really nice hotel—the type of place
you'd like to stay, if you came here—pool,
A/C in rooms. They want me to start working
within the week and I might, since my
tax refund is a debacle. Besides, I love
```

it here in Dahab. Each day, I make new
friends—both Egyptian and Western. The
pace of life and ocean view is all I could
ask for.

Yesterday was great. Since I'm now an
advanced diver, I went to Sharm el-Sheikh
to dive at the Thistlegorm--a British
transport ship that German bombers sank in
route to Saudi Arabia in 1942, during the
North African campaign. It was outstanding
to see. We were just under 100 feet and
the wreck was very well preserved. You
could see tanks, cranes, trucks, train
cars, locomotives, guns, motorcycles and
ammo. It was amazingly eerie. We finished
the day off with a dive at Shark Reef at
Ras Mohammed National Park, which had
amazing views of huge fish.

From: Brennan M Mulligan
To: Mom, Dad and Colin
6/10/01

Last night, just after midnight, Prateep,
a dive buddy and I climbed Mt. Sinai,
a pretty strenuous climb. At sunrise, we
awoke to pilgrims praying all around us,
and we felt a sense of community while
up there. There were unimaginable views of
the desert and I was surprised by some of
the people who made it up to 6500 feet. On
Wednesday, we will be leaving for Jordan.

I hope you enjoy the pictures I posted
and take them as an indication of how fun

things are over here--that I'm safe, happy
and in the company of a great group of
people. I've lost a bit of weight, as you
might be able to see, and I've grown quite
a mane.-b

Chapter 3

Mom's Turn

"…The real point of traveling is to discover oneself."

Despite my reservations about Bregenz, the Queen Elizabeth's departure resembled an MGM production with tugboats pushing, pulling, tooting, and standing by, as our great weight inched through the harbor. After the lifeboat drill, we raced around the elegant ship like little kids, running up and down staircases, and wandering through dark-paneled corridors. This was the "Golden Age" of sailing, so as third class passengers, our freedom onboard was limited. Yet, due to so few first class passengers, some boundaries were occasionally crossed—on both sides of the divide.

On our first night at sea, we ran into a storm that packed a wallop. Around 2 a.m., as the ship pitched and rolled, a china cabinet outside our stateroom tipped over and crashed. When we looked out, two stewards were already in the corridor sweeping up shattered glass and broken china. In the morning, the sun was shining, but the sea was still turbulent. Since neither Pam, my roommate, nor I had gotten seasick, we were among the few at breakfast. My friend Margaret also showed up, but she was so seasick, her skin was green, and she quickly excused herself. Around the empty dining room, cheerful waiters doused tablecloths with pitchers of water to keep dishes and silverware from sliding off.

Posted from the ship

Five days later, on the sunny morning of September 28, the ship sailed into Cherbourg, France. I remember being surprised that this busy seaport town looked nothing like my image of France. However, a large bus was waiting to escort us to "real France," Paris. On the way, we passed rural towns, and villages and a WWII cemetery. Along with being late September when most of the harvest was in, much of the picturesque Normandy countryside that exists today hadn't yet recovered from German fortifications and Allied bombs. We stopped in Rouen for lunch, reaching Paris—and the Hotel Isle de St. Louis—late that evening.

Paris! I spent two magical days sightseeing and searching for outdoor cafes where Hemingway, James Baldwin and their writing pals might frequent. I tried, but couldn't tolerate Gauloises cigarettes; *vin rouge* was even worse, but a strong cup of *cafe au lait*—also a new experience—passed the taste test, if I added gobs of sugar. We walked along the Seine, strolled through the *Folies Bergere*, toured Notre Dame Cathedral and Versailles' Hall of Mirrors. At the Louvre, I stared, from a foot away at *Mona Lisa.* The painting was surprisingly small; her smile familiar. There were as yet no jostling crowds, or timed tickets. No selfie sticks, or bulletproof glass covering her face; only a few of us students and a handful of tourists.

It took our bus another day and a night to travel through Switzerland and Germany. In Austria, on steep emerald green hillsides, billy goats grazed at impossibly steep angles. Once in Bregenz, I was enthralled. It's a picture postcard town; a hidden-away jewel nestled in the Alps. The Pfander Mountain hovered over the town, placing the ski lift just minutes away. A walk in the opposite direction brings you to Lake Constance, also called the Bodensee, the third largest lake in Europe, and a popular recreational area that borders Austria, Germany and Switzerland.

Also, a short distance from our home base—the stately Weisses Kreutz Hotel, where the top two floors had been converted into dormitory space—was the oldest part of town and the business district, where we discovered bakeries with *linzer torte* and apple *strudels* that we washed down with hot chocolate topped *mit schlag*—cream.

Without television or American newspapers, the world and worries I left across the Atlantic receded, and I opened my eyes on a new world and a host of magical experiences.

I traveled throughout Europe; several outings were school sponsored events, including our ski trip to St. Moritz, Switzerland. Because I'd never heard of St. Moritz, it was months before I knew we'd been skiing at a posh winter playground for wealthy Europeans and famous Americans like Elizabeth Taylor. But, the Alps are an equal opportunity playground, so despite sleeping in a modest youth hostel, we had full access to the enchanted mountains and savored the same panoramas as the glitterati.

One night in February, during *Fasching*—the Austrian version of *Mardi Gras*—I dressed as a boy and hiked up to a party on the Pfander. Besides borrowing one of the guy's jackets, I trimmed the ends of my hair, glued on a mustache and stuffed my hair under a stocking cap. The scene in the rustic old tavern was *Gemütlichkeit*— that uniquely German word describing coziness and comfort. There was a warm fire, a wood-beamed ceiling, a handful of Americans, rosy-cheeked Austrians, and one black girl, all having fun. Some of us were in costume; most were knocking back beers and getting drunker as the evening wound down.

By that point in the year, I'd already witnessed an ugly Bavarian bar scene in a Munich *Rathskeller*—a room dug deep into the bowels of an historic 18th century building. It was a grotto-like cavern with rock walls, a gigantic fireplace, endless pitchers of beer and too many drunks, one of whom abruptly brought our evening to an end when he stood up and hurled a heavy beer stein into the fireplace. For a stunned moment, I thought it might be a German ritual (it wasn't), like you see at Jewish weddings, when the groom stomps on and crushes a glass, symbolizing the Temple's destruction.

So, that night up on the Pfander, when the party suddenly got wobbly, my friends Margaret, Susan and I headed back down the mountain. Susan, a motherly type, was an engaged nurse from Queens, who had left her fiancé behind. Determined to see the world before settling down, she was also earning her last credits for a BS degree.

The air was crisp and clear with star clusters lighting our way. About a 100 feet along the snowy road, some guy, whose face I never saw, thought I was really a boy, and tackled me into a snowbank. Hearing indignant, high-pitched yelps changed his mind about further attack and he quickly helped me up and apologized in embarrassed English. I can only speculate why he singled me out. Because I was black? Because I dared to "have" two pretty girls to myself? Or, maybe no other American male, who had possibly pissed him off in the tavern, was in sight. So, he picked a fight with the first American "guy" he saw. Whatever the reason, my costume was obviously very convincing.

I don't recall any of us ever abusing our welcome to Bregenz, or seriously challenging local custom, except with Fraulein Gassner, our house mother, who was constantly aghast at how much freedom America girls were used to. However, I think small things sometimes raised eyebrows, including those of *gymnasium* students whose teachers also taught our college classes. When we met a teacher on the street, we greeted him with, "Hi Herr Schmidt" (or Herr Bauer, etc.). Addressing him in that manner was not intended as disrespect, although I think we annoyed locals kids with our easy-breezy familiarity and casual mannerisms.

Bregenz is not a large place. Today, less than 30,000 people call it home. I don't know what the population was in 1964, but it was small enough that 50 American students readily stood out. Around town, when patronizing shops and businesses, I occasionally heard the words "*die Schwarzer*," meaning the black girl, or black person. It can be used pejoratively, and I could never tell if it was. I know I was a curiosity, but whatever the older Austrians felt, besides freedom to openly stare, I was treated like everyone else.

We had only been there a short time when a local guy came to the hotel wanting to meet me. Vernfried was a baker's son; tall, ruggedly good looking, he spoke a little English, had a Beatles haircut and always wore a brown suede jacket. On our first date, he took me to dinner on the Pfander Mountain in his prized possession, a new car. By spending time with locals, I observed some of their everyday practices. Most homes still didn't have central heating and people often didn't use deodorant. Also, Austrians, unlike Americans, took exceptional care of their personal belongings.

With Vernfried

The evening we ate dinner on the mountain, Vernfried's car got stuck in mud. To free it, he retrieved clean, well-oiled tire chains from a purple velvet bag in his car trunk and used the chains for traction. Once free, he wiped the chains in snow, before carefully wrapping them in a cloth to take home and thoroughly wash.

A few weeks later, Georg (pronounced Ghee-org), another Austrian visitor came calling. I'm sure these guys came by, in part, because I was this curiosity, although I was young then, and generally considered attractive. But, I don't recall any other girls in our group ever dating local guys. Georg was three years younger than I, and still attended the local *gymnasium*. He was painfully shy and seemed to lack self-confidence. He spoke English fairly well, but often avoided eye contact when he talked, which he did sparingly and sometimes while staring at his feet. His lack of artifice was charming, though he occasionally spoiled it. Once he stepped on my foot and instead of just saying excuse me, he looked like he wanted to die.

Unlike Vernfreid's working class background, Georg was a descendent of the Hapsburgs who, until the end of WWI, still ruled Austria. He invited me to Sunday dinner with his family in their large timber and stucco home. And though his parents were lively and youthful, their wood-paneled house was dark and somber. Dressed with baronial furnishings, and ancestral portraits, it felt like an ancient relative's house, which it probably was. In contrast to their Bregenz home, Georg and I drove one Saturday morning, along with his older brother (who had a driver's license and whose name I've forgotten), to a luxuriously furnished apartment in Munich. The unit, especially the kitchen and appliances, was high-tech and futuristic-looking, like IKEA kitchens of today, but this was before many people outside of Sweden even heard of IKEA.

I'm not sure whose home it was, but the brothers treated it like theirs, confidently rustling up a simple lunch of cheese, preserves and hard crackers from the fridge. Before we left, I used the bathroom, which was handsomely tiled, with a fancy bidet, and other high-end fixtures. As mentioned, Austrians took great care with their belongings, but even the affluent reverted to bare necessity when nature called. There was no toilet paper in the bathroom. But, on the floor, beneath the empty toilet paper holder, was a stack of torn-up newspaper, something I'd never seen before, or used. Fortunately, I always carried tissues in my purse, so I didn't use newspaper that day, and still haven't had the pleasure.

It was never clear to me why we drove to Munich, about two hours each way. The boys didn't tend to any business, or household chores that I could discern. Without saying so, I think Georg just wanted to show me the apartment, which I was happy to see.

––––––

About two weeks after Munich, Georg invited me to go skiing on the Pfander, which sounded like the coolest date ever. Most of us Americans didn't ski as often as we liked. Many weekends were devoted to travel. On weekdays the sun set early, plus there was always something to do: go to the bank, or the cleaners, find a dentist in town, do homework. Also, I had my part time job, doing clerical work, two afternoons a week in Dr. Pinette's office.

As Georg and I set out, I looked forward to using new skills. By then, I was a confident advanced-beginner-to-intermediate skier and wasn't afraid of steeper hills, as long as there was some maneuverability. Georg, or course, had been skiing since he could walk.

At the top, he headed to an unfamiliar area, free of tracks, with fresh powder and ideal conditions, but a narrower slope than I liked. On the trail below, pine trees were buried in snow, well up into their branches. Overhead, the slate sky made it a dreary day, and around us, outcroppings and cliff-like overhangs were all heavy with snow. The weather had not been very cold, although I'd learn that, partly due to the lake effect, it was rarely bitter cold in Bregenz. I didn't know the mountain temperature, or conditions, but this section was steep and we would be passing beneath those snow-ladened out-croppings. The thought of avalanche didn't seem too far-fetched.

Without much ado, Georg took off like the expert he was. For me, the snowplow formation didn't work because the slope wasn't wide enough. My best bet was squatting low, skis parallel, but as far apart as possible, while taking as wide a turn as possible. It was soon obvious that Georg had chosen one of the steepest, narrowest, most advanced, and scariest trails on the mountain; and I had no business being on it.

But, skiing is exhilarating and we were moving fast. Despite a niggling sense of fear, at some subconscious level I felt pretty good shushing down the trail without falling. But not once did Georg check to see if I was okay, offer a word of encouragement or a safety technique. Then, he suddenly did one of those power twist and turn-stops—the kind of move that looks real cool and sprays eight feet of snow into the air. I thought he was taking a break. Instead, he looked my way, skied ahead, then took a flying leap and disappeared into the fog.

We'd come to a shelf on the mountain where the trail separated and the only way forward was to jump. I couldn't have told you then, and I certainly can't now, if the distance down was five, ten or fifteen feet. I can tell you that, as an amateur who was out of her depth, what I saw was leg-breaking terrifying. There was no chance to backtrack or find another route. I didn't know where I was, and it had started lightly snowing, so I did what Georg did, skied ahead, and jumped. Everything happened so fast; I didn't have time to pray, but Jesus and the snow angels were looking after me. I landed with my knees deeply bent, butt hugging the back of my skis that wobbled, but miraculously remained mostly straight.

After landing, there was nothing else to fear, because the slope widened and I could see to the bottom. Had Georg realized that I could have been seriously hurt, even killed by the stunt he'd just pulled? His behavior was so out of the ordinary that I couldn't explain it. Had he been showing off? Trying to show me up? I knew he was immature, but this put him somewhere between infantile and asshole.

––––––––

When comparing my Bregenz experience, with my husband's steadfast dislike of travel (especially if it involves a plane), it's no surprise that I'm the one who instilled a passion for exploration and adventure in my sons. How could I not, after falling in love with it myself? For Mike, however, white-knuckling-it, hardly describes his fear of flying. Some years ago, his work required frequent air travel. Before one flight, he tried tanking up at an airport bar. That backfired because, when he got to Seattle, he's sure the client smelled beer on his breath, and was no longer interested in Mike's brilliant idea. Next, he sought relief from a hypnotist. Hypnosis was a bit more effective. Now, instead of losing his mind when turbulence kicks in at

30,000 feet, he only maintains a death grip on his armrests and starts cursing under his breath.

————

Brennan and Colin's first solo travel was to YMCA Camp Lakewood, in Potosi, MO. Later camp experiences took them far and wide. From letters, I knew they toughed-out homesickness, used humor to deal with abrasive rules, and found joy with new friends from distant lands. Canoeing, waterskiing, rope and rock climbing were among new skills they mastered. Several experiences had a marked effect on improving their foreign language proficiency. Most importantly, they gained independence, and the self-confidence to keep testing new ventures. I just never imagined that this sense of freedom would lead to unbridled globetrotting.

Dear Mom,

Camp is fun, I am writing after church, for some reason I feel like writing. ~~you could~~

I am having a great time at camp and I am almost always busy exept weekends.

There is going to be a camp dance pretty soon. I am going to ask a columbian girl named Billie who is in equestrian camp. Write soon,

As Ever,
Colin

P.S. If at all posible please try and send a camera with film becaus̶ ̶I̶ ̶w̶a̶n̶t̶ to take pictures of th

Mike and kay Mulligan
6256 Fauquier
St. Louis Mo. 63105

A letter from camp

Chapter 4

Luck Can Be Quite the Equalizer

```
Brennan M Mulligan
To: Mike Mulligan 6/14/01
Re: pics
```

Dad–

Thanks for the message. I am now in Jordan and just got back from my first day of exploring Petra. Truly amazing--at least 10 times as cool as the pyramids with tons to see and do. I think Petra hasn't gained the reputation of the pyramids because it was only "rediscovered" about 150 or so years ago. Also, it's kind of out of the way, where the pyramids, literally sit at the edge of Cairo.

In the movie "Indiana Jones and the Last Crusade," there is a shot where Harrison Ford and Sean Connery are riding into what is supposedly the lost city of Alexandretta—a Hollywood embellishment of history. The shot is actually from the entrance to the lost city--a stunning walk through a desert canyon with walls 100 yards high on each side. Then the canyon opens up to this majestic structure that was literally carved out of the rock wall.

Canyon and Lost City at Petra

So far Jordan has been very impressive. The current king, Abdullah, essentially was raised as a westerner and English is his first language. The country is very westernized compared to Egypt. No more hustle or pushy salesman—a real relief.

 Take care,
-b

From: Michael Mulligan
Brennan M Mulligan
6/15/01
Re: pics

I've just printed a couple of the pictures you forwarded for
your mom. Her email is always breaking down. She said
she's happy you and Prateep are traveling together.

Prateep, Moose and Brennan

Your mom and I went to a huge wedding this weekend. All
kinds of local celebrities, although no sports stars. Art, our
old neighbor, and his Soulard Blues Band was one of several bands. The others emphasized Motown, but Art and his
guys acquitted themselves well.

Colin really likes your apartment. He also really likes having your car. We are thinking of you. Love,
Dad

To: Brennan
From: Mom
June 17, 2001
Brennan,

Yesterday, I spoke to Carol, my old roommate who now lives in Jerusalem. She hopes you get to Jerusalem. I hope so too, because it's an amazing city. Your state tax return came, and I'll deposit it tomorrow. Again, write me through Colin. Dad is in and out of town. It's been re-assuring to hear that you and Prateep are visiting major landmarks, and that you aren't off alone somewhere in the desert. Love, Mom

From: Brennan M Mulligan
6/18/01
Re: this one's for mom

Mom (and Colin by proxy),

I am fine. Things here are really good. Something great happened the other night at Petra. We met some Bedouin guys who offered to cook for us if we bought the food. We wound up having a night to remember. The Bedouins helped Prateep and me climb up to a spot where they hang out and the cops had no chance of finding them. We helped them set a fire and they cooked chicken and vegetables for dinner. The Bedouins were also able to get a bottle of whiskey with the money we gave them (about $8 between the 2 of us).

```
Everything is going to be okay here. Stop
worrying...seriously. I'll write when I
get to Amman.

Love,
-b
```

Brennan
From: Mom
June 19, 2001

I just checked my email, and happily, it's working
again; at least for now. I got your message to dad about
being in Petra, how beautiful it is, etc. Did you get my
message about obeying Petra and Jordanian laws and
rules?!

You have a summons to appear in court on August
2nd for that city earnings tax you never paid! That is
really ridiculous, since it goes back to 1999. If you don't
appear, they issue a warrant for your arrest. Try sending
me a short message, but anything important should go
to dad.

Love,
Mom

———

Before heading to Damascus, Syria, Brennan and Prateep spent
the third week of May in, and around, Amman, Jordan including a
side trip to the Dead Sea, about a half hour away. Due to unrest in
Israel, he said they had the beach to themselves, except for two guys
who got in trouble, and had to be helped out of the water because
they... "were screaming like banshees in Arabic and kept dragging

each other down while trying to stay afloat in 3-4 feet of water. We grabbed them and yelled to calm down and stand up. They finally did, and then we helped them out and got fresh water to wash out their eyes. At lunch, Teep and I had to wonder how two guys almost drowned, not only in shallow water, but the most buoyant water in the world…"

Later, at the Jordan Bar, they ran into a group of "annoying" Irish flight attendants from Royal Jordanian Airlines, who "had shitty attitudes and acted like they were too cool to be stuck in Jordan." But, they also met Melanie and Kelly, both Australian, who invited them to a party at the Australian Embassy.

At the Irish Pub, the next day, near Embassy Row, some high school kids were celebrating their graduation. "Besides boozing," Brennan explained, "they were unique because they spoke English like native speakers, with little knowledge of Arabic and almost all are heading to the US for college." The Irish Pub was also a hangout for ex-pats, and where TJ, a former US Embassy staffer, told them about a phenomenon called honor killings.

"It usually happens when a female in the family has sex out of wedlock. TJ said there had been 7 of these killings in the 20 days before we arrived in Amman. It struck me that there isn't much honor in honor killings. He said the killers usually aren't prosecuted because it's generally considered a righteous thing to do. Prateep and I wondered if TJ was full of shit."

The guys got to Damascus on the 24th of May, and loved it, especially the beautiful old parts. They found a "cool hostel called the Al-Haramein Hotel, and were sharing a 4-person room with Charlie and Jane," who were on a month long backpacking experience through the Middle East, and were my age. Brennan said he was eating well, and described a meal of shish-tawook, salads, hummus, bread, sauces and cooked vegetables.

At the Umayyad Mosque (maybe Islam's 3rd holiest site, after Mecca and Medina), he said:

Worshipers were amazingly welcoming, even though he and Prateep had on jeans and T-shirts. They sat on the floor, observing people praying, taking naps and hanging out with their families. "Mosque visits are so interesting," Brennan wrote, "because I know little about Islam, but from observations, the religious rituals and culture are so different from my background."

To: Brennan
From: Mom
6/26/01

It is wonderful that you are in Damascus. Thank you for putting my mind at ease about your safety. I'm sorry to be such a worrier and I'll try to stop, especially since you used up all your email time reassuring me, instead of only talking about the wonderful experiences you're having.

It is expensive there? Sophisticated like Amman, or not? It surprises me that most of the tourists are American, instead of Australian or European. Again, I feel very comfortable and happy that you're visiting metropolitan areas. When you first left home, I imaged you in remote destinations where help, should you need it, was far away, and where being alone could be dangerous. Everything here is same old, same old. Stay in touch. Have fun.

Love, Mom

To: Brennan
From: Mom
6/27/01

   I wish you had a camera. Is it out of the question
to buy one? It's too bad you and Prateep can't keep
traveling together, because it seems to be enriching
the experience for you both. And of course, two guys
together are safer than one alone. Your last email was
special, but you didn't answer my question about how
you're feeling. I was concerned about the weight loss.
I don't imagine you're eating the portions we eat here
and there's no pantry with chocolate chip cookies. But
are you feeling well?
Take care.
Love, Mom

Brennan M Mulligan
6/26/01 9:06AM

Mom—

I feel fine, and I'm eating natural
portions here just like I've always done.
True, there's not as much snacking and I
do a lot of walking and sweating which
also causes weight to drop off. I think
most of the weight came off during my
"water works" period in Egypt. There was a
time when I seriously wondered if I'd ever
take a solid dump again—but enough about
that (by the way, I am "solid" once again.

Egyptian cuisine has been a regular topic of conversation with people along the way. At some point, unless you're staying at a 5-star place, you're going to get the runs. Period. There's absolutely no way to avoid it. If you're like me and had no choice but to keep eating the food, then you just keep getting sick until your system recovers.

Hygiene in Egyptian kitchens runs from atrocious to just plain awful (except of course at 5-star places). I have a hilarious story in my journal about finding a roach in my spaghetti one night in Hurghada (it sure doesn't sound funny, but you'll just have to trust me). For some reason, the virtues of sterilization just haven't been realized there yet. I'll just say that both Jordan and Syria have been much (much, much) cleaner. -b

■

Chapter 5

What Happens in the Alps...

Like Brennan, who prefers traveling with a friend, when I was in Bregenz, and ever since, I've vacationed with a companion, or in a group. For me, more than my sons, it was a matter of safety. But, when my strong, strapping sons read about the wacky 507 mile road trip I took to Holland in 1964, I can see them scratching their heads wondering why I worried so much when they traveled. I think the answer is multi-pronged. I was generally a cautious kid, but I was only 20 years-old, and research on adolescent brains didn't conclude that only male brains take longer to mature. Sure, the world has always been dangerous, but not in the inexplicable, violent ways we see today.

Something extra kicks in when I travel—when many of us travel—an undaunted spirit, that sense of adventure. I'm afraid of deep water (I can swim, but not well), yet willingly stepped into a tippy kayak to traverse the icy waters around Skagway, Alaska. On the Atlantic Ocean, in Mexico, Carol, my roommate and I paid a few peso to sail, without life jackets, on a rickety little sailboat, because we felt sorry for the young pilot, whose cheerful disposition was at odds with his stunted, malnourished body. Afterwards, Carol and I averted our eyes when his mother showed up to beat and curse him for wasting time with the *chicas*.

Why did I do these things that were so out of character? Timing, a desire to try some right-brain quirkiness, and knowing I'd never return to a place, also led me to hold a swarming beehive without cover-up equipment, because the beekeeper said it was safe. Plus, I knew that I'd never want to do it again. On that same trip, a snake handler draped his six foot boa constrictor around my neck, because on that day, I wasn't afraid of the snake.

Terry with boa constrictor

In Bregenz, Dr. Pinette occasionally granted us a long weekend, so we could travel. Amsterdam, with its storied windmills and meandering canals that stood in place of some city streets and avenues, was on my wish list; and I especially wanted to visit Anne Frank's house. So, along with my giggly friend and fellow student, Brian, I made plans to hitchhike 820 Km (507 miles) to Amsterdam from Bregenz, Austria.

Besides being inexpensive transportation, female hitchhikers were an anomaly and I reasoned, that would help us quickly flag down cars. Secondly, in town, or walking to class, we mostly wore knee socks, unlike European girls who wisely wore tights in cold weather. Our knee socks served as a beacon, especially for older ladies who passionately pointed and "No-no-ed" when they passed us on the street. At first, I assumed they saw it as daring and risqué—too much skin showing. Later, when an elderly woman pantomimed a shiver, I realized that all grandma-types were the same. Mine back home railed against me going bare-legged, unless it was the height of summer.

Sometimes, standing out from the pack was not a bad thing. Actually, I kind of had a trifecta-thing going—black, female, American. Many residents of Vorarlberg, that conservative, tucked-away southwest arm of Austria, where it meets Lichtenstein, Germany, Italy and Switzerland, had likely never seen a woman who looked like me. Perhaps black soldiers had shipped into these parts during WWII, or an African student studying in Munich might have taken a sightseeing tour to this picturesque portion of Europe. Possibly, the only stranger sight, especially in Germany or Austria, would have been a white man or woman standing on the road, who could somehow be identified as Jewish.

That was another thing about the locals. Since WWII ended, talking about Jews or uttering the word *Juden* or Jew was flirting with the *verboten*. Once, in a conversation with Vernfried about our director's pretty redheaded secretary, he wondrously whispered the word *Juden*, because rumor had it she was partly Jewish.

If there was any downside to the Holland trip, it was that Brian probably wasn't the best guy to team with, but he was the available male. As a tall Nordic, baby-faced, willowy blond, Brian just didn't look serious, and he never was; about anything. The term gaydar hadn't yet been coined, but few, if any among our group of students didn't suspect that he wasn't gay. With Brian, I couldn't count on him not to make a joke or giggle if a dicey situation arose, which is exactly what happened on our first ride.

The driver, a blonde, blue-eyed, apple-cheeked, jolly-looking fellow was decked out in a felted-fedora and a handsome collarless, Tyrollean-styled boiled wool blazer with shiny coin buttons. He signaled that I should sit next to him in the middle front seat, with Brian on my right—a seating arrangement that several drivers would indicate. We took off and after a few minutes, the man merrily burst into song, while using his right elbow to brush against my left breast. Crossing my arms didn't entirely discourage him. I leaned into Brian, and sure enough, he started giggling.

Maybe it was youth, or naiveté, but today I'm amazed that escalating or imminent danger was not my primary concern, so I must have found some comfort in Brian's presence. Still, with a creep on one side and a clown on the other, I wanted to get out of the car, but figuring out how was the problem.

At the end of 2017, the issue of women being sexually harassed or assaulted suddenly took on enormous prominence, first in

America, then worldwide. While reading these stories I, like women everywhere, thought of harassers I'd encountered, and that 1964 driver was one of them. In all of these cases, there's a question of why we didn't fight back. I abhor violence and ugly confrontation, plus I'm sure I didn't want to seem rude or ungrateful to our "nice host" for giving us a ride. It never crossed my mind that he was probably ten steps ahead of me, had it all planned out, and felt entitled to feel me up, because I had willingly gotten into his car.

Why was I brave enough to cuddle with a boa constrictor, and get close and personal with a hive of bees, but couldn't speak up for my right not to be mauled? Because that's how I, and tens of millions of other women are programmed. We aren't supposed to rock the boat, or cause an embarrassing scene. Doing so might make us look bad, or ungrateful, or we might get fired, demoted, or maybe it was all "a misunderstanding." But, times are changing. Through the courts, the news media and social media, women are signaling that sexual harassment now has consequences.

Fortunately, before we got to the German border, just eight miles from Bregenz, Mr. Alpine Predator solved my problem by pulling over, letting us out and waving a cheery *auf wiedersehen* before exiting the Autobahn. Brian and I had a good tension-releasing laugh about it and I couldn't berate Brian for being Brian.

After that ride, the day went more smoothly and, as hoped, the next car to come along usually stopped. Traffic was sparse on the German Autobahn, a newly built superhighway that had no speed limit then. In the post-war economy, Germany was still rebuilding, but several manufacturers built cars with powerful engines. On that road trip, we frequently sped along at 160 kilometers an hour, thus making excellent time. But when threatening gray clouds, that had stalked us all day, turned to rain, our luck ran out because drivers don't like wet hitchhikers in their cars.

Fortunately, a series of inviting lights, about a mile up the road, turned out to be from a small regional airport, probably somewhere between Frankfurt and Dusseldorf. It was only about 5:00 or 6:00 p.m., and despite being all lit up, the place was deserted and flights had halted for the day. Gratefully, we stretched out on a row of seats, until a guard, and not a friendly one, came over and asked, "*Was machst du hier?*" Neither of us expected a deserted airport, nor to be confronted about sleeping in seats that no one wanted. In America, passengers routinely sprawled across airport seats or slept on the floor. Brian, usually not shy about challenging authority, was at a loss for words. In desperation, I blurted out a whopper. "We got dropped off early and our flight leaves in the morning." The guard understood English quite well because he said, "You can't sleep in the airport." Thank God, he didn't say we had to leave. So, there we sat all night, pretending not to be wet, exhausted and hungry, until a tinge of pink awoke in the sky, and we slipped out into the damp, foggy morning.

When we arrived in Amsterdam the next evening, we'd been on the road for 33 hours. A pedestrian directed us to a street with a row of attached, four story buildings, with steep front steps that reminded me of Harlem brownstones. Some were hotels. We stopped at the one with a green neon, Rooms for Rent sign. The brilliant color looked welcoming but, by then, we didn't care if the rooms were monkey cages, as long they had beds. We were exhausted, but eagerly rushed up the steps and into a front room with a black Naugahyde bar that resembled the ones in some cheesy basement Rathskellers back in the States, which, in the 1960-70s, were all the rage. Propped on the two available bar stools, with drinks in their hands, was a black American GI and a coarse-looking blonde, her legs crossed, one high heel dangling, and wearing enough makeup to be a kabuki dancer. No one said anything, but the look she gave us was somewhere between a "come hither" and a smirk. This was one time that Brian didn't giggle. We both just turned around and left.

■

Chapter 6

The Ride Turned Out Wild

Traveling is such a wondrous experience.

On 6/29/01, Brennan wrote that Beirut was very westernized, but a pepperoni pizza from Dominos wasn't as good as home. A doctor prescribed antibiotic eye drops to clear up Prateep's advanced conjunctivitis, and they were sharing a 3-person room at Pension Home Valery with Neville, a carpenter from Ireland who was doing a two month Middle Eastern tour.

"At dinner," Brennan wrote, "we met a local beauty, Suha and her friend, Fatima. I ended up going out with Suha, with Prateep and Neville in tow. Suha later invited us all to dinner with her mother, sister and brother, for a delicious meal of salad, cooked vegetables with a beef and rice dish wrapped in cabbage leaves. Ultimately, their hospitality made us uncomfortable. They're immigrants from Algeria, of Moroccan descent, and obviously didn't have a lot of money (her dad died a few years ago), but were emptying their cupboards to feed us.

"Suha was great. She's beautiful, kind, considerate and intelligent with good character, but she's from a different world with a different set of values. She's Muslim and her family's unspoken expectation that I was a potential husband, after only a few days, made me slightly uneasy. So, that's my news from the past few days."

```
To: Mom
From: Brennan
6/30/2001

We've been walking around Beirut, eating
lemon freezes and arranging a side trip to
Quneitra, which required permission from
the tightly secured Ministry of Tourism.
Later, at the US Embassy, where we hoped
to watch some ESPN, we only got to talk
with a Syrian guy through bulletproof
glass. Unlike other embassies, ours is
surrounded by high fences and razor wire.

The next day, we headed to the town of
Quneitra, an outdoor memorial to the
1967 Six Day War, that's just 1 Km from
the Golan Heights. Much of Quneitra was
destroyed, but the gutted hospital stood
out most starkly.
```

Bombed hospital

We missed the yelling matches that occur
between civilians on both sides of the
divide, but saw a lot of armed security—
Syrian police units and UN troops.
Quneitra is a governorate bordering
Lebanon, Jordan and Israel. Life goes on
in small towns in the distance, and on the
Israeli side, there are well-irrigated
fields with crops growing.

The Syrian view of the war states that
the town was intact, but destroyed by the
"Zionist Aggressors" when they withdrew to
the Golan Heights. My guess is that the
Israeli version of the story would differ
somewhat.
Brennan

To: Brennan
From: Mom
July 6, 2001

Our phone was out for a full day and a half, and I was
sad not to wish you a happy July 4th. You being in countries that suffer or are at war makes being an American
very meaningful. Did you get new contacts? Is Lebanon
(and was Syria) as reasonable to live in as Egypt? Is the
food better? The same? Love, Mom

―――――――

To: Mom
From: Brennan
July 7, 2001

Beirut was really fun, mostly for its
night life. Now, we're in Tripoli, and
I finally sent the souvenirs I've been
lugging around since Egypt. The statues
are from Yusuf and Mahmoud's family to
ours. The camera has some pictures of the
pyramids and a bunch of Hamadi--a cool
little kid in Luxor. Hamadi was pretty
interested in messing with the camera, so
I just let him run with it. One of the
papyrus scrolls I sent has the names of
everyone in the family (Mom, Dad, Colin
and me), written in hieroglyphics. The guy
at the shop was pretty much a complete
dick, though.

Here in Tripoli, scars from the war remain
throughout the city. I couldn't help
wondering what life was like during the
16 years of fighting. It must have been
surreal—in a bad way, of course.

From: Michael Mulligan
To: Brennan M Mulligan
Mon, Jul 9, 2001
Re: parcel

I want to apologize for my silence over the last few weeks.
I have been regularly reading your mails to your mom and
Colin, and following your itinerary. I just have not written—
mostly because there hasn't been much to talk about.

Since we've never been there, your mother and I are going
to Las Vegas for our anniversary. We are also going to
Chicago for a few days at the end of July, for a combination
of business and pleasure. It is some big time hot here, but I
guess you're getting some of that where you are, too. Keep
writing. Your letters make interesting reading, aside from
the fact that we love hearing from you.

Love, Dad

To: Brennan
From: Mom
July 10, 2001

Hi Brennan,
The package arrived today. The galebaya and turban
will make great Halloween or costume party outfits. I
know just where I want to put one of the vases. Does it
matter who gets which one? I'll take the camera in to
see what we can get. It's so tiny, can't you find another
one to take more of these incredible sights you're seeing? By the way, Colin seems to have a new girlfriend.
Her name is Jenny. Also, did you get new contacts?
Love,
Mom

From: Brennan Mulligan
7/11/01

Mom—

Hello from Aleppo. Prateep and I are
at our last stop together. He's been a
great travel companion. In a couple days,
Prateep will head into Turkey, about 100
Km north. I'll fast-track back south to
Dahab, about 10 times further. On our
way north, we ended up in Homs, after a
wild bus ride, because we didn't know the
difference between Homs and Hama.

Here, in Aleppo's center of town, where
we're staying, many buildings are
centuries old. The area reminds me of
some four-story buildings in the Central
West End, in St. Louis—small hotels and
apartments with balconies, and businesses
at ground level. During the day, busy
outdoor cafes have the mellow vibe of the
CWE.

Yesterday, we visited Aleppo's Citadel. It
dates back to the 3rd Century and towers
over the Old City. It was like being in
some pharaoh or emperor's castle, which
it was in ancient times. In rural areas,
we've driven by villages with olive trees
that would pass the two century mark.

I'm excited about returning to Dahab
to start working on the dive master
certificate. It's hard to describe how
happy I am with the way things have been

these past few months. After all the
struggles and despair, the clouds have
finally cleared. I'm right where I want
to be. I've been doing a lot of smiling
lately and it feels great.

Love, -b

To: Brennan
From: Mom
July 11, 2001

I'm thrilled you're feeling so happy, but hadn't realized
you'd been struggling and in despair. On this trip, things
have worked out well for you, but it makes me sad that
you felt the need to take off for unknown parts to find
peace and happiness. You weren't very forthcoming
before you left, but I thought (maybe I hoped) you were
undecided about career choices, and just needed some
space and a vacation, of sorts. I wish we could talk.

Love,
Mom

From: Brennan M Mulligan
7/12/01

Mom-

First, I had another eye exam done because
it was free and my new contacts match
the same numbers you sent. My plan is to
arrive in St. Louis on October 7th--a week
before the Wolffman's wedding. That also
gets me home before Thanksgiving, which
should make you happy.

Regarding the "despair" comment. Don't
think that I'm not satisfied with how
things have worked out over the past
few months, but in my view I survived a
somewhat tough process (much of it to do
with a lack of closure after the breakup
with Shelly). Also, Grandpa had just
died, which was hard for me, and I was
reeling from the Alamo building purchase
that almost bankrupted me and Schake.
Fortunately, our little real estate
investment has stabilized.

I'm eager to move forward with a number
of things: continue "career development"
as a computer professional, use my scuba
certification when I travel (to hopefully
offset expenses), and continue to improve
what Schake and I started. We'll be able
to talk at length when I get home, but I
hope you're happy with this synopsis for
now.
Take care. Love,
-b

```
From: Brennan M Mulligan
7/13/01

Mom—
Last night, Teep and I had to haul ass to
the bus station; hilarious, with us saying
our goodbyes while running at a full
sprint. At the last minute, I learned that
the regular midnight bus to Amman actually
left at 11 p.m.

Me: (gasping for breath): "Somehow it
seems right that we should say goodbye
this way."

Ice Teep (equally exhausted): "So, anyway,
it's been real."
```

———

Two months later, on 9/11/01 Brennan was back in Dahab, enjoying a last hurrah with his scuba buddies, when two jetliners flew into New York's World Trade Center and a third plane hit the Pentagon. By the time a fourth jet crashed into a field near a strip mine in Pennsylvania, the "Al Queda-Terrorists-Thousands-dead" drumbeat began.

After binge-watching live TV, the enormity of what I was seeing shifted to horror. Was this, I wondered, the start of WWIII? So far, Americans abroad weren't a priority, but increasingly, I feared for Brennan's safety and hoped his Egyptian friends would protect him if he became a target of these extremists. Phone lines and Internet connections were overwhelmed. On Wednesday, an email from him finally popped up in my inbox:

September 12, 2001
Mom, Dad, and Colin,

I continue to be shocked and saddened
by what I'm seeing on TV and reading in
the news. What kind of people would do
such a thing—or find such a thing good or
necessary?

If there is a Middle Eastern link to
yesterday's events, I can't help but
think of all I've seen and experienced on
this trip. Many people in the West view
this region as inherently hostile towards
them. In my experience that couldn't
be further from the truth. As word
spreads of the attacks, I continue to be
approached by tons of Egyptians, Bedouin,
Sudanese and Westerners alike, who know
I'm American and want to genuinely offer
their sympathies. It's humbling to feel
the kindness of these strangers, yet my
thoughts are now with people at home.

In a real and horrible way, much that I
have witnessed and learned on this trip
could be relevant in what's bound to be
an ongoing national discussion about the
world in which we now live. As I sit near
the end of what's been a great, even epic
adventure, it is unfortunately tarnished
with a very ugly backdrop.

I'm deeply saddened, but eager to move
on and not let evil influence the quality
of life in our country. It will be good
to get back and catch up. I'm thankful

that everyone in the family and our close
friends seem to be okay. I'll look forward
to seeing everybody soon. Take care of
yourselves...
Love, -b

To: Brennan
From: Mom
September 13, 2001

What a relief to get your email and learn that you're
safe!! Some mothers will never hear from their child. I'm
eternally grateful that I did. Marilyn called and said Liz
has been crying because she's so afraid for you. I'll let
her know you're okay. In fact, from what you describe,
you might be safer over there, than we are here. Nerves
are still jangled, and anxiety remains high. Even though
planes have been grounded, I keep looking up at the sky
wondering if some other evil is going to rain down on us.

I better keep this short, because I have a lot of people
to call, including Dad, to let them know I heard from
you. I'll write more soon. Take care. We love you and miss
you.
Mom

From: Brennan
9/13/01 7:53AM
Re: More news

Mom-

Since I returned to Egypt, I have had
Sinai-only visas, only good for 2 weeks at
a time—thus, I've traveled to Eilat, in

Israel, every 2 weeks, for visa renewal.
But, now that Israel closed its border, I
cannot get another visa, so leaving the
country is my only option. I am required
to leave by a week from Saturday, but I'll
likely be gone before then.

As for flights or places to fly from, Sharm
el-Sheikh, the city at the southern tip of
the Sinai Peninsula, is my only option. I
can only move between Taba (this side of
the Israeli border) and Sharm. There are
tons of flights between Sharm and Western
Europe, so I'll look to make my way out
that way, and wait until trans-Atlantic
flights start up.

I may spend some time around Europe
(perhaps visiting some folks I've met on
this trip who are now home). In other news,
I got an email from some of the Penn crew
in New York. Apparently a guy named Chris
Stothard who was a couple classes ahead
of me is unaccounted for. Another guy, Joe
Reda, who worked in the World Trade Center
was on his way to work and had to run for
his life, as he turned a corner and saw the
building falling towards him. He ran at a
full sprint for 6 blocks to the waterfront
and jumped on a subway to Brooklyn and then
Queens. Quite amazing.

Keep in touch and stay strong. Things here
are fine, but I haven't stopped thinking
about everyone at home.

Love, b

September 14
To Brennan
From Mom

Hi,

    I'm sorry that you can't get to Jerusalem to visit Carol and Micha, but it sounds like you've made peace with coming home. I often hear from friends and acquaintances that their kids come back somewhat, to greatly changed from this kind of travel experience. Besides being relaxed and content, I hope you've found something deeper to hold on to. Take care. We love you and miss you.
Mom

———

Three weeks later, when Brennan got home I was giddy with relief. He looked tired, thinner and subdued. And, after a half year in Saharan sunshine, his dark brown hair was streaked with killer blond highlights.

Brennan returned to a nation brimming with Kumbaya moments and patriotic unity. Still, it didn't take long to see how six months of "dropping out" had changed him. He seemed surprised that the world he'd left still moved at a fast clip. His friends worked all day or attended school, and didn't have time to play, or listen to stories about Bedouin bracelet girls, or Chico, the finger-tapping guitarist. For a while, Brennan moved back in with us, but his head and a piece of his heart remained elsewhere.

Later that fall, when his high school football team went to state finals, Brennan didn't sit with his old teammates. Some of these young men were more like brothers to him than ex-schoolmates. Segregating himself high up in the arena, he avoided them. Because Brennan had changed, I don't think he was ready to find out how the old gang fit into his life anymore. In the Middle East, Brennan bonded with a different team—young men and women to whom he entrusted his life. He'd lived minimally, owned two just two sets of clothes, had few decisions to make, and no mother telling him to turn down the music.

I get it when soldiers return to war zones again and again; being a hero is appealing. You just have to avoid the next IED or bullet. Rock solid buddies have your back. They're easier to live with than whiny kids, demanding wives, and shallow friends who make it easy to forego the easy life for one of risk.

For Brennan, it wasn't just old friendships that took time to re-process. After 9/11 our economy, much like the World Trade Center, collapsed. Easy job pickings also disappeared. In this go-round, he didn't find employment for months. It took longer to secure his footing and to let go of the life he left behind.

Brennan ended up following his passion, a career in computers, where he landed on a sweet spot.

He spends his days in cyberspace, working with numbers and formulas that turn into something I don't understand. Today he lives in St. Louis and Patty, a significant other, has entered his life. He continues to travel when he can, including revisiting Dahab, and later Greece, where he hooked up with Prateep, Moose and her husband, Costas, all Dahab dive buddies.

Remember Brennan's habit of traveling abroad with little money? About three years after Egypt, on a planned two week stay in England, Brennan landed at London's Gatwick Airport without a plan, or a place to stay and with only a $100 in his wallet. Officials detained him. Initially, it looked like they weren't cool about admitting kids who seemed aimless and/or broke, or else they didn't give a damn whether he had an ATM card in his wallet or not.

The phone is on my side of the bed and it's never good to hear it ring at one o'clock in the morning, but Brennan is very good at CWIT (communicating when in trouble).

"Mom, they won't let me into the country!"

"Brennan? What? Where are you? It's the middle of the night! Who won't let you into the country?"

"Customs guys. They won't let me leave this secured area to use an ATM machine to prove that I have money. They said I don't have sufficient funds or a place to stay for two weeks."

"I thought you were going to get in touch with Doug and see if you could start by spending a few days with him!"

"I was, and I want to, but I hadn't done it yet. They talked to Doug first and asked if he was expecting any friends from the US. He didn't know I was coming so they're trying to say I just made that up."

"Why hadn't you emailed him? Oh, never mind. So, what now?"

"I don't know. I think they're going to make me come home."

"Will you get a refund on your ticket?!"

"No!"

Within hours, they did fly him home on the first available plane that was heading to the States and no, they didn't give him a refund.

About a month later, Doug's mother, who'd learned of Brennan's ordeal, called to tell me that in the 1980s, Doug's London apartment had been an IRA hangout. The "Irish Troubles" had mostly ended, but, when Brennan—last name Mulligan—showed up with insufficient funds, and a cockeyed story relating to that particular apartment, he might have been flagged as a potential headache that Scotland Yard didn't want or need.

be made.

/2 - Beirut

Our trip to Damascus was uneventful aside from me trying to beat the shit out of one of the baggage handlers at bus station. This fucker was insisting on getting a backsheesh putting a sticker on my bag and putting it in the luggage hold the bus. I had a 100 fil coin on me which he wasn't interested in and the smallest cash note I had was a 5D note. He was only able to produce 2 JD in change yelled at him and called him a fucking cocksucker. It was a nice little scene, but I doubt many of the people fully understood the details of what I was saying. Somehow had to get my 3 JD's worth out of that backsheesh.

The next step for us was the ~~Baghdad~~ Al-aramein Hotel off the main drags in downtown Damascus. It was located on a quiet sidestreet that had ivy hanging overhead. The room we had was a 4-bed shared room that we took with Charlie and Jane married couple that are my parents' age who were enjoying a month-long backpacking experience in the Middle East now that their kids are all out of the house. The room provided welcome relief from the usually noisy streets of Damascus. Also, to the north of our hotel was a very old and european-looking series of streets to which the hotel's ivy covered street served as an entrance.

The old style streets continued pretty far to the north where we headed for drinks at the spot that was to become our watering hole and eatery - The Damascus Workers Club. There we helped ourselves to $.50 Baradas and a full spread of shish tawook, salads, hummus, bread, sauces and

...ed vegetables. The Workers Club comes highly recommended from t...
...nter.

I think one of the big reasons Prateep and I have got on so ...e past several weeks is that we both travel at about the same ... The focus of our travels is to soak up culture, hang out a... some partying in the various stops we make along the way... ...e both enjoy meeting other people to hang out or even travel ...th and of course we love the adventure that invariably comes ...h moving around for the first few times in a region such ... the Middle East.

That said, we haven't really been too busy making su... see every sight along the way. My approach has always ... ...t if there is a place worth seeing that is relatively easu... ...d painless to get to, then I will certainly make the eff... ...visit it. I have given up on seeing every pile of roc... ...re will be to see along the way here. Honestly, once you... ...n one pile of rocks, **PART 2** ...them all.

One sight we did ge... ...long the way was the Umayya... ...sque — a site that is second in holiness in the Muslim world ...ly to Mecca and Medina. In all I suppose we spent an ... ...r walking around the mosque, sitting inside and observing ...various people praying, relaxing, talking and hanging ou... ...th their families.

Mosque visits are truly interesting for me because I even a... ...s point I can still say I know very little about the ...trul tenets of Islam. In the almost 3 months that I ...ve been wandering through the region, I have certainly ...en my share of the culture that surrounds the religion ...cluding many of the religious rituals people go through ...gularly. I have also heard people give second-hand accou... ...what the Quran tries to teach, but I haven't been ...le to experience this first-hand because of my inability ...read arabic. Still, mosque visits give me an opport...

■

Chapter 7

Number Two and Deja Vu

*...each of them is contributing to a better world,
one...step at a time*

Eighteen months later, in 2003, when Colin announced that he too was planning to spend a year backpacking around the world, I thought, oh, sweet Jesus, here we go again. This time, an additional concern was the Iraq war. Both world, and US opinion of President Bush's decision to start that war hovered somewhere between dismay and, "Are you f*king' kidding me?"

I searched for an upside to Colin traveling and living among people who seethed with resentment towards America. One comfort was the four productive years he'd just spent as a high school teacher, administrator and coach. Along the way, he'd earned a master's degree in Middle Eastern studies. So, I reasoned, after pushing so hard, this time off could be beneficial. Additionally, I hoped that exploring the world might enhance his knowledge and chances of getting into one of the select PhD programs he was applying to. For weeks, Colin worked to setup online bill-paying accounts, and get his house and affairs in order. His tenants' rent would cover the monthly mortgage with enough left over to finance the trip. Miles, aka, Suitcase, his eighteen pound cat, was coming to live with us.

"Mom," he said, a few days before his August 1st departure, "everything's almost done, although I won't have time to complete my grad school applications and essay before I leave on Thursday. But, no problem; they have Internet cafes all over the world. I'll write it while I'm traveling."

Oh, God, I thought, these boys are killing me.

———

COPENHAGEN
From: Colin Mulligan
Date: August 12, 2003
To: Terry Mulligan
Subject: On Vacation

Hey,
By the way, I'm in Copenhagen, not Oslo, and this is not a vacation, but now for business stuff.

Thanks for taking care of so many details. Ok, first of all, it figures with that health club. I can't believe I ever got involved with those assholes. One big headache after another. Glad to be done with them. You should tell them to go piss up a rope. Don't sweat the grad school stuff right now. I won't start worrying about that until November, so you shouldn't give it a second thought either.

Ok, I'm having a great time and a good deal of the reason that I'm able to is because of you. Thanks for helping me out. I love you.
colin

From: Colin Mulligan
Date: August 18 2003
To: Terry Mulligan
Subject: Osman
Hey--

Today I had one of those encounters that makes me know this trip was meant to be.

I was eating lunch in the park and this guy, Osman, a Turkish Kurd, walked over and asked if he could join me. I said yes, then told him I'd been to Turkey, enjoyed it, and had read a lot about US relations with the Muslim world. We began to chat in earnest and I could tell he really wanted me to know he wasn't stupid. He was keen on talking about his favorite book: "The 100: A Ranking of the Most Influential Persons in History." Apparently, the Prophet Mohammed is at the top of this list, two places higher than Jesus, an obvious source of pride for my new friend.

At one point he paused. 'I want to say something to you, but I am afraid it will make you angry.' I told him to please speak freely. 'The US will never win in Iraq,' he said, 'because the men they fight are doing God's work!' He launched into a bit of a tirade. He had had almost no formal education. Most of his information came from the Internet, but he was a voracious reader, also incredibly bright. He spoke flawless English and gave every indication of being a hard-working and determined young man. Yet he was grateful to find someone who listened to his words, without dismissing him as just another poor uneducated immigrant.

He clearly approved of the ambush tactics being used against Western forces in Iraq, but said he did not support the murder of noncombatants, women or children. Osman wasn't a violent man, yet his combination of spiritual vigor and socio-economic frustration made me question if his love for Islam could ever be manipulated into hatred that burned deep enough to make him a killer. I was struck by just how thin the line between disaffected young Muslim and unrepentant terrorist might be.

Okay, a line's building and I have a lot more surfing to do. Talk to you later.
colin

To: Colin
Date: August 19, 2003
From: Terry Mulligan
Subject: Passport

American Airlines mailed your license. You must have left it at the airport. That reminds me; you should make extra copies of your passport page and send me one too.

Mom

To: Colin Mulligan
August 19 2003
From: Terry Mulligan
Re: SOFTWARE

WHERE ARE MY COMPUTER SOFTWARE DISCS?
THEY'RE NOT BACK ON MY DESK!!

To: Terry Mulligan
Date: August 27 2003
Subject: Plans
Hey Guys--

It's very easy to forget your 'other life' while
relaxing in the warm Greek sun, speaking of which,
it was very chilly today. I'm in Gotenburg, Sweden
and I was in the sun shivering in my fleece. That
was nice of American airlines to mail my license
back, but I checked twice and they told me it was
gone.

Good idea about sending you a copy of my passport.
I'm having a great time, but I miss you guys; stay
in touch...
c

To: Terry Mulligan
Date August 31 2003
From: Colin Mulligan
Subject: Plans

I do have a plan! I'm in Tallinn, Estonia and have met up with my first travel buddy, an Australian named Tarun. We met on the top deck of the overnight ferry from Stockholm to Tallinn, and celebrated his twenty-fifth birthday with a bottle of red wine and a shared joint. Mom, before you freak, they didn't throw us overboard for smoking one lousy joint.

Tarun and I will probably stay together for at least a week. We're both heading south through the Baltics--into Lithuania, then to Eastern Europe. We'll part in Krakow, and I'll move on to Munich to meet Aggalia for Octoberfest.

As for your computer's software, I can't be very specific, but I know where it is. It's in one of the boxes that I put in my basement storeroom first. I used a box that used to hold paper. It's in the back-middle of the storage room, but there'll probably be some pretty heavy stuff on top of it. You might need to get Dad or Brennan over there to help you move a dresser and the sofa. Take whatever you want/need.
c

From: Colin Mulligan
Date: Thur Sept 1, 2003
To: Terry Mulligan
Subject: Re: GREs

What the fuck on the GRE?! I was positive that
I knocked the essay portion out of the park! The
explanation they provided succinctly demonstrates
the problem I have with that stupid test. Pardon my
French, but it truly pisses me off that some dumb
fucking desk jockey gets to read my essay and
have such a substantial say in my academic future.

Satisfactory analysis of complex ideas, my f-ing ass.
Well, in case you couldn't guess, being on the road
isn't helping my language. I know I didn't prepare
for the test as comprehensively as most people, but
that score makes it sound like I'm a goddamned
moron. Anyway, I could go on and on about this,
but I'm not quite ready to buy their assessment of
my abilities.

I have not done any actual written work on my
personal statement, though I am perpetually
composing in my head. I think that I will most
likely mail it from South Africa. I can't wait to get
to Africa. I hear the bush calling me.

To: Colin Mulligan
Sept 4 2003
From: Terry Mulligan
Re: Motherly advice that I hope you will take

As a consequence of the GRE score, I think it's important to nail your personal statement. Your percentages were also so-so. And, you have to write the thing, not just think about it. Didn't you say it was due next month?!

Even though they want your sofa, the tenants are only halfheartedly trying to arrange for me to get into the storage room. If they ever make up their minds, maybe I can dig out my software, you know!! Trying to get Brennan or Dad over there when it's convenient for everyone is like herding two year-olds. Truthfully, I'm not sure I want to see the inside of your house. Mom

From: Colin Mulligan
Date: Sat Sept 6, 2003
To: Terry Mulligan
Re: hey all

Riga was not at the top of my list, but I LOVE Riga. It's unlike any place that I've been. To make things even better, I found a kick-ass place to stay with lots of fellow travelers. I'm writing an article about it. Stay tuned.

From: Colin Mulligan
Sept 10, 2003
To: Terry Mulligan
Subject: A piece I wrote about Riga, Latvia

by the way, i'm not using any more capital letters.
they take too long to type and that costs more.

after my experiences in sweden and estonia, which,
with a few notable exceptions, were disappointing, i
was starting to question the wisdom of my chosen
path through europe. although i can safely say
that these doubts were poorly founded. riga is an
amazing place, well worth the wait.

the 20th century was not kind to the baltics,
and the scars of latvia's past brutalization are
everywhere. it's quite apparent that the end
of soviet occupation and the promise of e.u.
membership have revitalized this country, and there
is an unmistakable sense of hope for the future,
yet all is not well. latvia's turbulent past has taken
its toll on the population, and this is evidenced by
truly shocking levels of alcoholism, poverty and the
strong grip of post-soviet gangsterism. i have yet
to distinguish between young punks trying to look
tough, and truly sinister characters, but i'm not in a
hurry to find out. they don't seem to be interested
in poor, unglamorous, short-stay backpacker-types,
anyway.

the new climate of optimism does not always
translate into opportunity, and life here is often
tinged with depression. the other day, a man died

on the street outside the bus station, less than a block from our hostel. i wasn't there, but jeff (he's also staying at my hostel), described the scene in detail. the man's body lay there for some time, and only his head was covered with a plastic bag until he was picked up, unceremoniously deposited into a makeshift hearse and carted off to the morgue. on this block, there is a nonstop flurry of activity--the grand outdoor market, taxis, streetcars and pedestrians--but i can't help thinking that it would be a lonely place to die.

i'm not exactly sure why the death of a man i didn't know, and never saw, has stayed with me but i think it has something to do with how he represents the riga that i have come to know. amidst all the hustle and liveliness, it's easy to forget about those who are suffering. as i sip my tea and 65-cent beers, talk with friends and stuff myself with meat and potato pancakes, i can't help feeling like the scores of pedestrians who walked past this man's body, paying him only passing attention. and so it goes here, the days easing by with an intoxicating combination of excitement, hope, danger and tragedy. hope you liked it.
c

From: Terry Mulligan
Date: Sept 25, 2003
To: Colin Mulligan
Subject: Your Tenants

Do you just hop on a train and go where it's going? I didn't know this part of Northern Europe was on your itinerary. But, it sounds exciting and off the beaten track. Summer is about over. Any frost yet? It cooled off here after three, much needed days of soaking rain.

Did you stay hooked up with the Aussie fellow? I still haven't sent you the analysis of your GRE scores. Before you get completely out of preparing-for-grad-school-mode, don't forget to work on your personal statement.

Despite your track record, your GRE writing sample wasn't that great, so, a strong statement is definitely needed. I never asked—did you go out partying, or something, the night before the exam? Good on the passport copy, now send it to me.
Love, Mom

From: Mike Mulligan
Date: 9/27/2003
To: Colin Mulligan
Re: Prodigal's Dad

It's me. It's been more than a month and a half since you left, and this is my first letter. Not a good example. It's not like I haven't been thinking about you though. Quite the contrary; it's just hard to get a feel for the little keys on my Blackberry, my toy a client gave me because he could never reach me.

The other day, I came across that CD you burned for me. My favorite is about a guy who is asking someone to tell his girlfriend goodbye. He knows that's weak, but he cannot bear to see her again to tell her himself. Brennan said it was a Don McLean song. Anyway, when I listen to the CD, it makes me think of you.

I hope all continues to go well for you and that the trip is fulfilling your expectations. Mom's email is still not working right, but said she liked your piece about Riga, but would really like to read your personal statement.
Take care,
Dad

From: Colin Mulligan
Date: 9/28/2003
To: Mike Mulligan
Subject: Prodigal's Dad

hey dad,
rest assured that i am taking good care of myself (for the most part) and eating well. there is a huge market here with plenty of delicious fruits and vegetables and a cheap cafe downstairs from the hostel.

I just got back from the airport seeing Aggalia off. It was a bit sad, but nothing like the goodbye in st. louis. i found a great hostel in munich, less than a five minute walk from the oktoberfest festivities, and full of friendly, outgoing young people from all over the world. anyway that's all for now. i am very grateful that life is so good. lots of hugs.
keep in touch,
colin

From: Colin Mulligan
Date: 9/29/2003
To: Terry Mulligan
Subject: Re: Auschwitz

yesterday, just after dawn, i took a train to the town of oswiecim, which the germans called auschwitz. regular people live here now, so I can see why they use the polish name. it was about a 30 minute walk from the train station to auschwitz, which is the more 'museum-y' part. there are photos of when the jews had just arrived and had their heads shaved, and stacks of hair piled up, and contraband rooms. it's about another 20 minutes to birkenau, where endless rows of bunkhouses remain.

mom, it's not like when you were a student here in the sixties. now there are lots of jewish groups walking around, carrying israeli flags and accompanied by security guards. the grounds and fences are well maintained but the barracks have started to rust, peel, etc. there's debate about whether to spruce it up (and look too nice) or let it continue to decay (and risk collapse).

the ovens were dynamited when the nazis fled from the soviets, but a pond at birkenau is filled with ashes from the crematoria. it was a windy, overcast day and a fitting atmosphere for imagining the atrocities that took place on these grounds. i never thought i'd see this nazi killing field.

in comparison, krakow is a beautiful city with a
historic central square, and amazing architecture. so
far, i've hung out in an underground brewery, seen
a street art exhibition and had a lot of good food.
it's a university town, so it's pretty liberal here, also
cosmopolitan. i like it a lot.
c

■

Chapter 8

Interconnection of Learning

Before going abroad to Bregenz, I remember telling my music professor that his class complemented readings in my world history text. He seemed pleased and said something like: "You're experiencing the interconnection of learning; you'll make those associations again and again." My professor was right—textbooks, novels, and lectures set the table for a year of memorable new experiences.

The Diary of Anne Frank was on my mind when I walked silently through the hallowed grounds of Dachau Concentration Camp. We were the only ones there. Dachau was a small, seemingly emptied-out town, just north of Munich. The Nazis didn't imprison Anne at Dachau. They shipped her to Bergen-Belsen, where she died from tuberculosis, but for me, Anne gave substance to this death camp.

The room where I stood was large, with dingy, yellow-tiled walls; a place ordinary enough to defy the imagination. There were vents in the ceiling, and small metal openings scattered haphazardly along the walls, with drains in the floor. There was no tour guide, just the silence of us holding our breaths. If I hadn't known where we were, I would have thought I was inside the rundown remains of a large shower room, in what had once been a boys or girls summer camp, and not a Nazi gas chamber.

During our year abroad, little was left to chance. Besides that somber stop at Dachau, we visited other cities and towns in Germany, and traveled around Austria and Switzerland. By spring of 1965, after months of sightseeing, it felt like I'd walked every museum corridor in countries we visited, and dipped my fingers into enough holy water to be ordained an archangel in heaven. Dr. Pinette, our sage director, didn't agree and saved the best for last, and easily my favorite trip—Easter in Italy.

First stop, Milan, and a visit to Milan's enormous gothic cathedral. That evening, we attended an opera at world famous La Scala opera house. I can't remember what I saw, but do recall finding it so much more enjoyable than Wagner's *Flying Dutchman* at the Met, in NYC the previous year, which we'd been required to see for Music 101.

When we got to Pisa and saw the much anticipated Leaning Tower—in the 1960s, it leaned so much, the top was about 17 feet from the base—some students refused to climb up, fearing it could topple over. But, it wasn't until the late 1990s, when it got worse, that Italian officials temporarily closed the tower for shoring up and restoration.

Leaning Tower in 1964

In Florence, we had a day to visit dozens of jaw-dropping sites, while absorbing centuries of Medici family history, ancient architecture and fabulous art, including Michelangelo's *David*.

In the still prudish, 1960s, a sculpture like *David*, depicting a beautiful man's face and perfect sleek body, with equally flawless and larger than life genitals, was probably reason enough for some people to visit Italy. As I studied the figure, I remember trying to behave casually while sneaking peeks at other viewers to see if they were as astonished as I at such frank expression of the male figure. For all that the statue represents—Roman culture, artistic excellence, beauty—its sexuality cannot be ignored. I was not well versed in art, or knowledgeable about American museums, but I kept wondering if any in America would display this piece.

For me, Rome, despite its sprawling size and fifteen centuries of history, proved to be more compact and digestible than Florence. Instead of a thousand small bits, which were difficult to keep straight, Rome left sweeping impressions, and giant-size memories like the Vatican, St. Peter's Basilica, Michelangelo's Sistine Chapel, the Colosseum and the *Pieta*. In Rome, I felt the enormity of where I was, and that I was privileged to be there among so many treasures.

Next stop after Rome was Venice, but before Dr. Pinette cut us loose to explore outdoor cafes, or glide off in gondolas, he led us into St. Mark's Basilica, an elaborate, gothic-Byzantium cathedral. As our eyes adjusted to the dim lighting, we dutifully oohed and aahed at marble columns, saintly statues, elaborately designed 9th century prayer books, and the overhead splendor of encrusted gold mosaics in the domed ceiling.

Afterwards, in St Mark's Square, I had another "connectedness of learning" moment. Instead of people, the square was crawling with pigeons; more than I'd ever seen and that's a lot of pigeons when you're from New York City. Something about me attracted all the birds my way and they wouldn't be dissuaded. It was like being drawn into a scene from *The Birds*, with me trying to fight them off, while they aggressively swooped and dive bombed.

My salvation was an old man, a pigeon lover, who entered the square with a bag of seed and a magical device—a small handheld clicker—compelling the filthy fowl to waddle off and fly towards him. The whole scene with the birds, the Byzantine Basilica, and the picturesque plaza nuzzling against the placid lagoon, echoed Thomas Mann's novella, *Death in Venice*. In Mann's story, Gustav, a lonely and restless old man comes to Venice on vacation. Despite a threat of cholera, he remains after noticing the young boy, Tadzio, playing in the square. Gustav becomes obsessed with the child, spying on him, lusting after him.

St. Mark's Plaza with few pigeons

While looking around, I realized that Mann didn't just pluck the novella's setting or mood from thin air. He'd stood in this storied plaza and felt, or conjured up something tainted within the eternal dance of love and lust.

As I stood there, this ancient space was being sullied by a flock of hostile birds who frightened visitors, spread guano and encouraged another old man's obsession; small birds, instead of a small boy. Soon, the pack of pigeons thickened; crashing and smashing into each other, fighting to perch on the clicker's shoulders and head.

———

To: Colin Mulligan   October 15 2003
From: Terry Mulligan
Re: My trip

I've been wondering where you were. I guess you didn't get my message regarding concerns about South Africa. As for possibly meeting you there, I started researching in *Lonely Planet*'s guide, which was disconcerting because of dire warnings about S. African crime. *Lonely Planet* is not exactly directed at the meek traveler. Apparently, thieves and rapists get very lenient punishments, so they're bold and brazen. When you get there, be extremely careful. I'm also looking online at traditional tour groups. Most are pretty expensive. I'm still thinking this all out.
Mom

———

For the next month, before flying to Africa, Colin continued exploring Europe. His emails described snowcapped Alps in Gastein, Austria, a picturesque inn, and "kick-ass" beer. He found good laundromats, and met other backpackers, including two drunk Welsh guys who "blasted the pretentious, condescending, schoolmaster voice Tony Blair used to justify supporting the Iraq War."

Compared to the more conservative vibe in Southern Germany and Austria, he liked the cut-loose feel of Hamburg, a more liberal, Northern industrial port city. Bremen, he informed me, was the home of Beck's beer, and where two hilarious Scottish guys staying at his hostel were financing their trip by busking in the town square.

"I'm in Bruges," one email stated, "the Flemish part of Belgium. A man here spoke to me in Flemish and when I answered in French, he became annoyed. Apparently, the French/Flemish divide is quite a serious matter for some."

■

Chapter 9

Africa

The type of travelers…I like to call LJPT, locals just passing through

In early November, Colin landed in South Africa, where I arranged to meet him on the 16th. The travel agent planned an elaborate itinerary, starting with my non-stop, eighteen hour flight from Atlanta to Johannesburg. Life being what it is, I knew that after about eight hours of hang-time over earth, my husband would have had a nervous breakdown—or given me one. So, despite all the dire warnings about crime in South Africa, I jumped at the chance to head there and have Colin be my escort.

When I met him at the Portswood Hotel in Cape Town, it wasn't the noticeable body odor, the scruffy goatee, or even the peculiar looking dreadlocks that had just started knitting together, that scared me about what the next nine months might bring. It was his backpack. The large, over priced, but carefully selected REI water resistant travel pack with multiple compartments and lockable zippers that once contained essentials like camping equipment, toiletries, a water purifier and clothes, was gone. In its place was a small model like he'd carried in ninth grade. But, it wasn't even full.

———

Cape Town, November 17, 2003

The local time was 4 p.m., 26 hours after I'd awakened the previous day to start the 8500 mile journey. Despite an hour delay for the Secret Service to settle President George H.W. Bush aboard our plane, the flight was flawless with plenty of food and free drinks. I'd stayed awake all night, reading *Hawaii* by Michener, because I hadn't thought to buy *The Covenant*, which he set in South Africa. I finally fell asleep a few hours before arriving in Cape Town. By then, the plane was empty. I'd slept through the stop in Johannesburg, but when I awoke, I was pumped and ready to go. A short time later, Colin and I headed for the Waterfront.

November is early summer in that part of the world and the balmy weather was accessorized by the aqua-colored South Atlantic. Overhead, downy cumulus clouds rushed by propelled by the wind. We walked around the Victoria and Alfred Waterfront, which sits between Table Mountain—that I wish I'd had time to explore—and Robben Island, that I would visit the next day. Despite being a tourist haven, the Waterfront is also pleasantly walkable, and a charming, picturesque working harbor.

Some ten years earlier, South Africa had captured world attention during the violent end of Apartheid, along with centuries of racial oppression and brutality. I was on alert for the system's leftover slights that might be directed our way. But, with its cinematic views, trendy shops and ethnically diverse diners sipping lattes and crisp South African wines, there was no sign of that time.

Colin still had his convertible, zip-bottom pants. He needed a good shave and a buzz haircut. Since that wasn't happening, he settled for a new collared shirt. His other grimy clothes went to the hotel laundry.

Before leaving home, I'd made plans with Chuck and Ann Korr, friends from St. Louis. Chuck was a visiting professor at Cape Town's De Montfort University and had emailed me saying, "When you get here, you and your son must meet us at Camps Bay for a sundowner." Hmm, was a sundowner a drink or a view of the sunset? I learned, it can be both; a specialty cocktail, often made with Grand Marnier, cognac, lemon and orange juice. Reportedly, it tastes best while watching the sunset, which in Cape Town can be a near religious experience.

There are exceptions to the city's breathtaking beauty. One would be Khayelitsha, a large slum I saw when my plane flew in low over the outskirts of Cape Town. Later, in the Soweto section of Johannesburg, I would get up close and personal with another shantytown.

If you favor a hipper, more well-heeled crowd than at the Albert and Victoria Waterfront, it's the seaside area of Camps Bay. There I saw high-end restaurants, expensive boutiques and wealthy people living in hillside estates that overlook the ocean. Chuck and Ann pointed out the Twelve Apostles rock formation, a favorite look-see for tourists. Then, on the beach, we caught the last rays of sun, our sundowner, before adjourning for dinner at Pirana, a restaurant that served thin sliced tuna that was out of this world delicious.

————

The next morning I delicately reminded Colin that it was mid November, the time he'd set to get serious about finishing his grad school statement. "I have been working on it," he offered.

"Did you print it out?"

"No, it's expensive to print over here. I'm writing everything down on a legal pad first."

Well, okay. Under the circumstances, I reasoned, maybe long-hand was a thrifty and necessary way to approach this.

"May I read what you've written so far?"

He was lounging on his bed, reading a copy of *The Alchemist*, but reached into his backpack and dug out a grimy, dog-eared legal pad with three pages of writing that described his life's goals. Words failed me, but something my husband said months before, that I'd dismissed as nonsense, now swam back into view. I'd groused to Mike about how poorly Colin did on his GRE's, and was almost certain he hadn't cracked the prep book, nor opened the accompanying CD-ROM.

"Maybe," Mike said, "Colin doesn't really want to get a PhD."

———

Long Street was near the hostel where Colin had been staying in Cape Town; an area he described as having a lively night scene with dancing and music sounds spilling into the street. I just hoped to find a hair salon and zeroed-in on one that did braids. Kofi, a Cameroonian stylist, neatened-up Colin's dreads, but he slicked on so much bees wax, that before we left the salon, it started oozing down his face and neck. Alas, there wasn't much improvement.

Clothing was very inexpensive, so after lunch, I bought Colin a pair of pants and two new shirts. We made arrangements with Ann and Chuck to see a performance of "Cry the Beloved Country," and booked a next day wine tour to Stellenbosch, an old Dutch city. Last, was a stop at the Internet cafe so I could send a few emails and Colin could finally start typing his statement, even though he'd left it back at the hotel.

As we approached the store, I saw what could only be described as four of South Africa's throwaway children. Three little street urchins, about seven to ten years old, were wallowing on the ground, then intermittently stomping a fourth boy with lackadaisical vengeance.

They kicked and punched him in his back, his side, his head, then, seemingly exhausted, stopped. Their clothing, slick with dirt, blended with their dusty brown skin, as they lolled on the ground, then attacked again. Colin walked right past them. The Asian proprietor of the Internet cafe stood relaxing in the open doorway that exposed his computers to the elements. With hands in his pockets, he was looking the other way, as if he didn't see the children.

"Mom," Colin said, "you see this a lot in Cape Town. They sniff glue all day and he probably doesn't feel anything. If you chase them away, they go around the corner and do the same thing. Come on, let's go inside."

The store was empty of customers. Colin used one of two working computers and it, like all the machines, had rust around its frame. Having lost all interest in sending emails, I sat tensely, fearfully, watching through the open double doors, trying to understand how this beautiful city could allow these children to live like this.

———

The next morning, November 19th, I took the twenty-five minute catamaran ride to Robben Island, where Nelson Mandela was imprisoned for eighteen years. Colin, acting like a local, did not join me. He'd been taking scuba lessons and wanted to finish the last in a series he'd already paid for.

Much about post-Apartheid South Africa is hard to put your arms around. The former prisoners who lead these Robben Island tours are one such enigma. Our guide explained that he and other former inmates, much like Mandela, were committed to building the future, rather than dwelling on the past. When I visited, the island was a community of 130 people. Former black inmates and their white jailers, along with their families, now lived side by side; their kids attended the same island elementary school.

But, the visitor-friendly, neatly folded gray blanket inside Mandela's B section cell did not mask the specter of torture and sadism still hovering over these now spiffed-up barracks. Even in captivity, Apartheid had ruled. Punishments and privileges were doled out according to race; whites, coloreds, then black men at the bottom of the pecking order.

When Mandela was released in 1990, his eyesight had been compromised by conditions at the island's lime quarry. I soon saw why. For thirteen years he and other inmates spent their days mindlessly breaking up limestone rocks. They carried them to one end of the quarry, then back to where they started. Ocean breezes didn't reach into the stark white pit and the heat in there was intense. Sun reflecting off the white limestone scorches a person's eyeballs.

Mandela's cell

I had on prescription sunglasses and also used my hands as a shade visor; still, the sun was blinding. Mandela might have been lucky to retain any sight at all.

For centuries, the island held prisoners; also lepers, paupers and the mentally challenged. When standing at the shore, which is nine miles from the mainland, depending on your viewpoint, it's a Godforsaken island, nearly impossible to escape because it's surrounded by predator sharks, icy Atlantic waters and ferocious waves crashing onto jagged rocks. It's also a natural paradise for its other inhabitants: tortoises, penguins, and a variety of smaller birds and sea animals.

———

On Friday morning we flew to Johannesburg and, because our travel agent refused to book us in Johannesburg proper, we were driven twenty miles away, to the Holiday Inn in Sandton, a charming suburb with flowering Jacaranda trees and stately homes nestled behind ten foot-tall hedges. But, when you looked closely, the hedges were all topped with razor wire.

In my journal that first night, I wrote the following: "Here in Johannesburg/Sandton, you don't always get service with a smile, or friendly answers to questions, as we did in Cape Town." The hotel check-in clerks, both black, were either in way in over their heads, or after years of oppression, were extracting revenge on the "rich white (and black) people" who stayed here. I thought the white guy in front of us, who was trying to check-out to catch his flight, showed extraordinary restraint in not jumping the counter and pounding the crap out of them both. Colin and I were in no hurry, nevertheless both attendants were infuriating—heads down, at times immobile, seemingly deaf, maybe lost in a whirlwind of new technology, or perhaps some memory of the past was just too raw for them to indulge in courtesies.

In the morning, the first of several riveting sights was in Soweto Township, with its miles of mountainous toxic waste, dirt and rock. These 20-40 foot tall peaks stood along the streets, in place of buildings found in most metropolitan locations. Hundreds of these eyesores were leftover slag from many years of gold mining. Along with most of its gold, Johannesburg's ravished, earth-toned townships had also been stripped of most greenery and trees. Some of what remained in this mining area were hostels—barracks-type living quarters sitting on barren brown land. These shelters were for the few miners, some of whom now bring their families, who come in from the bush to work in what's left of active gold mines.

We briefly visited Freedom Square, the location of the 1976 student uprising. The just-opened museum was named in honor of thirteen year-old, Hector Pieterson, the first student to be shot by police. The museum was still evolving, but photos and a video documented the slaughter—a savagery condemned by the world—that many credit with finally breaking the back of Apartheid.

I was shocked that our next stop was Soweto's sprawling shantytown, an area crammed with rickety squatters shacks, extending as far as the eye could see. During Apartheid, this neighborhood was sometimes shown on American television as an example of how intolerable life was for black South Africans. Residents here had no running water or electricity, except for some who attach long cords to the electrical source, then run the wires over rooftops and down the sides of a few buildings.

We stopped at one of the tiniest shanties—the size of a double refrigerator carton, and not much sturdier. Almost all these places were jerry-rigged with mismatched wood, tin, plastic, and cardboard. A few more prosperous residents lived in small modest, unpainted wooded homes that had shingled roofs.

Our guide, Sello, an educated young black man, respectfully acknowledged the elderly gentleman who lived in the refrigerator box-size home, politely addressing him by his last name. I imagined that Sello's deference to the residents of this modest neighborhood was why they tolerated gawking tourists. It also occurred to me that the people might get some remittance from the tour company. Still, I was embarrassed for intruding into the simple lives of these strangers, most of whom were elderly or infirm, and obviously poor.

Soweto is short for Southwest Township, and within it, there's Soweto's shantytown, and the "Beverly Hills" of Soweto, where opulent mansions stand. However, most of the neighborhood looked like a typical middle class suburban community with traditionally built homes. Two such residences belonged to Reverend Desmond Tutu, and Nelson Mandela. We spent about a half hour at Mandela's house, in what felt like a totally laid-back visit to a friend's home, including using the bathroom.

Mandela's bedroom

A man sitting in the den, talking to a friend, was a house sitter-security-guide person. When I asked him if Mandela and Winnie had lived there together (by then they were divorced, Mandela had remarried and Winnie's reputation was tarnished), the guide went into a passionate defense of Winnie's activism, and her sacrifices to gain freedom for black South Africans. He told me that the inside bathroom had been an add-on, so Winnie wouldn't get shot using the outdoor toilet. As we were leaving he added one more thing—the public still greatly admired her.

————

Our visit to a bustling outdoor market in Soweto is just one of many stops to savor on this trip. It was there I met the little medicine man. His corner card table was located next to a large thriving butcher's display of three full-sized, skinned cows, hanging from a horizontal pole. With the sun shining brightly on the meat, it seemed voyeuristic to gawk at warmed beef that I thought might prove toxic to the people buying it, so I scooted over to the squat, gray-bearded medicine man and was rewarded with a big gummy smile. Unlike the butchers, who juggled an avid clientele, along with hordes of flies at their stall, no one paid any attention to the healer, whom I suspected had once been important.

Despite his tattered overalls and plaid shirt, I assumed he hadn't always dressed that way, and pictured him wearing tribal clothing. This man was one of many people I wish I'd photographed, but, each time I reached for my camera case, Colin, who I'd obviously taught well, kept nagging me and saying, "Mom, stop. Don't be an ugly American. You can't just take pictures of people."

The medicine man's small corner card table was "decorated" with a couple of old, 6.5 ounce Coke bottles filled with twigs and leaves, that I supposed were herbs and potions. But, truthfully, it was hard to discern much of anything except dirt inside the scratched, cloudy bottles that looked about as old as Africa.

"What are your medicines for?" I asked him. He pointed to three, and through a thick, toothless accent, I heard "impotence" and "crying babies." I couldn't understand what was in the third bottle.

I considered buying something, but the grime and grit put me off. Also, I'm superstitious and the whole setup made me think of "The Gods Must be Crazy," the South African movie about a Co-ca-Cola bottle falling from the sky. It lands in the Kalahari Desert, where a bushman picks it up. He then has nothing but misfortune as he sets out on a venture that will take him to "the ends of the earth," so he can dispose of that bad luck-bottle that looked just like the coke bottles on that table.

It was also at this market stop that a young, white Brazilian woman, a CPA, in Johannesburg for a conference, latched onto me—literally. She hadn't gotten out of the van at our other stops and was clearly afraid at this noisy marketplace, swarming with dark skinned people. No other whites were in sight, except a couple from our van. Because I was older than everyone in our van, I think she took me as a mother figure and I was happy to help her walk among black Africans, who were just like me, Colin, and her—"Except," I jokingly told her, "they speak with an accent, like you do." We linked arms and she relaxed and grew more at ease.

■

Chapter 10

Meeting Robert

On Sunday morning, November 23, Colin and I waited in the Holiday Inn lobby for a new guide who would drive us to our next adventure, a safari in Kruger National Park, about 4 ½ hours away. After a week in South Africa, I couldn't stop people-watching, and marveling at how well the multiracial transition was generally working since Apartheid's end. South African guides go through rigorous training, and all seemed to follow certain protocols, so I was looking for someone in the signature white polo shirt and tan or navy pants. But then, Robert walked into the lobby and headed our way. Picture a 5' 9"-ish, splay-footed white guy with a barrel chest, buzz haircut, a dead eye, bad teeth, and wearing khaki shorts, a sports logo tee-shirt, aviator sunglasses, and sandals.

"My van's right outside. Is this all your luggage?" he asked, assertively pointing to my suitcase. Colin, seemingly unperturbed, hitched on his backpack. Under my breath, I muttered, "Jesus, holy Christ. Did they send a Boer skinhead as our guide?!"

"By the way, I'm Robert M," Skinhead said, "and you must be Terry, and this is Colin. A pleasure to meet you." Colin took the front seat; I sat in back and Robert didn't stop talking for the next three and a half hours. He told us that Johannesburg elevation is as high as Denver's, that the country only has 1% of forest land, and because labor is so cheap, all new houses, even modest homes, have "servants quarters," which are needed to sell the property.

Along the way, Robert pointed out a Taiwanese township, and told us about a secret organization of white supremacist Afrikaners called the Brudabot who still exist on a small scale. He showed us two types of invasive trees: the black wattel and jacaranda, and explained that the vibrant red-colored soil in the area we were passing through came from iron nutrients. He taught us ten Zulu words, and gave an etiquette lesson: stay seated when someone enters the room, but greet them with an open hand and avoid direct eye contact. One of several "Oh, wows" occurred when Robert said, "No, that strange looking bush is not a type of giant pineapple, it's an aloe tree."

Our schooling continued through the Eastern Transvaal and across the fertile valley along the Batutti Mountain Range, until we reached the Malelane Sun Hotel, which reminded me of scenes from the movie, "Out of Africa." Each "room," situated along a winding garden path, resembled a thatched roof hut. Around us, birds chirped and twittered unfamiliar melodies and, to eliminate any doubt about a familiar screeching and chattering sound, a sign on our hut's door read, "Mind the monkeys. Keep your doors closed."

Our "hut" in the bush

By then, I was loving our offbeat guide, whose stream of chatter was like a piñata gushing out goodies. The sun was fading, but before Robert took the evening and next day off, he gave us a quick twilight tour of Kruger. With all things South African, Robert was a knowledgeable guide, including animal facts. To my surprise, my favorite part of that evening was my introduction to new exotic bird species.

With Robert

After dinner, Colin and I relaxed on the game viewing deck. While he stood at the rail, watching something below us, I sipped a cold South Africa chardonnay and brought my journal up to date. "Mom." Colin called, after about twenty minutes, "check this out." Besides hippos and rhinos in the spotlighted river below, that I'd already seen, Colin pointed to an epic battle taking place. I'd missed

109

a few body parts, but a grossly engorged python had what looked like a gila monster's leg and foot, in its mouth.

The more complete and much anticipated safari tour of the 20,000 sq. Km refuge (the size of the Netherlands) began the next morning, at 4:45 am, with Louie as our guide. A former banker, Louie undertook this new line of work after Apartheid, when a black man replaced him at the bank. The first thing I noticed was that our safari vehicle was open-sided; like totally open to the elements—and the animals. As for our safari, the best way to describe it is to say, if you're able to, take your own African safari; words are inadequate. Face-to-face exposure to giant beasts, in their native habitat, is unlike anything in zoos. And to be honest, the underlying anxiety that comes with exploring in open-air vehicles adds to the thrill.

In Kruger, popular lore states that visitors should see "The magnificent six:" the lion, leopard, rhino, elephant, hippo, and cheetah. We never spotted a cheetah, but missing one elusive big cat paled in comparison to the unexpected pleasure of observing dozens of gorgeous birds gracefully flying and strutting their stuff.

Growing up, my bird exposure had been sadly limited to loathsome aggressive pigeons. It took this trip to help me understand why people go gaga over bird watching, and that they travel to far away places like Kruger Park to indulge their passion.

That morning in Africa, among the colors I spotted were bright yellow, royal blue, and aquamarine-colored birds; they came in large and baby sizes. Some were noisy, like the gray lourie, known as the "go-away" bird because of the sound it makes. Others had long lovely tails or showgirl head feathers. I bought a bird book and proudly kept track of my sightings. Once back home, I purchased a hummingbird feeder for my backyard.

All this is not to minimize the animal kingdom's power brokers—three curious elephants who momentarily blocked the road while they checked us out; a lion pride, their faces and paws bloodied from the kill, feeding on a giraffe; and the fantastic, prehistoric-looking black rhino, that Louie warned was bad tempered and more apt to charge than the less common white rhinos, or other large beasts.

That evening we took another twilight tour with Lawrence, a black guide. Apologizing for hardly spotting any animals, he instead beguiled us with tales of danger and death. On a small bridge, he let everyone out of the truck, then informed us that last year, three people were killed, including a guide who was attacked at this same spot by a stealthy leopard who'd been hiding under the bridge. With that same scenario playing out—the animals seemingly avoiding us—I was sufficiently spooked and eager to head back.

Rhinos

With reluctance, we left Kruger on November 25th and crossed into Mozambique. After, about a mile along a desolate stretch of road, a policeman with a rifle suddenly stepped out of the bushes in front of our car.

"Passports," he demanded. More startled than frightened, I wondered if he assumed Robert and I were a couple and had a problem with that. Instead, he looked at the passports and, in perfect English and obvious suspicion, zeroed in on Colin and me.

"You two have the same last names! Why is that so?" He directed the question to me.

"Yes, he's my son."

"But, he's younger than you are," he remarked, seemingly not caring that mothers are older than their children, or else not believing me.

"How is that the case?"

I spelled it out for him. "We have the same last names because I am his mo-ther," I said succinctly. "He is my son. We're both named Mulligan, because we have my hus-band's last name. This man," I pointed to Robert, "is our guide and I'm sitting in the front with him, because the seat is more comfortable up here. I go back home to the States in three days and my son will continue his travels in Africa." Since the policeman kept that awestruck look on his face, I still wasn't sure if he believed me, but he stepped aside to let us continue into Mozambique.

Robert was continually educating us on the good, bad and ugly in Africa. A few days earlier, he'd pointed out a young girl with a man, whom he thought might be a sex trafficker. He'd then explained, "There is a lot of that kind of thing in this part of the world."

"Sorry," I said, looking over at Robert. "I know you told us to let you do the talking if we were stopped. But, what on earth was that all about? Did he think I was a pedophile or Colin's sugar mama? Totally gross," I added. "But, how did I do? Did I say the right things?"

"You were fine. He could have been looking for someone transporting a girl into Mozambique. Maybe it was on his mind. I wouldn't worry about it."

———

As we left the wilderness and neared Maputo, Mozambique's capital, Robert pointed behind us and said, "We've passed the landmine zone." He further explained that after Mozambique's independence from Portugal, in 1975, two internal Mozambican factions, the Renamo and Frelimo began a protracted civil war that didn't end until 1992. Millions of people died—from brutality, starvation, and some from the 28 million landmines planted throughout the country. Many mines remained, including those in the uninhabited area we'd just traveled. It occurred to me that all that empty space could easily entice an unsuspecting camper to stop for the night, pitch his tent, and end up dead.

Maputo still showed signs of the war, most noticeably in unoccupied bullet-scarred buildings, some without windows, and others missing chunks of stone or brick. Men in wheelchairs had one or both legs missing. Rightly or wrongly, I attributed their disfigurement to the proliferation of those landmines.

In small serious ways, Maputo still seemed to be at war with itself. Sections of the city were no photo, no pedestrian, and no stopping zones, including the street where the president lived. But the city also showed signs of revival. It was the last night of Ramadan, and families were feasting and celebrating along the beachfront. New restaurants had blossomed; some with plain, utilitarian decor—one looked like a reclaimed warehouse—a la SoHo hipster-style. But these no-frills buildings with cavernous spaces and mismatched furniture had their own cachet, plus delicious food at reasonable prices.

Besides piles of freshly caught seafood, uncrowded white sand beaches, and striking colonial architecture, such as the Museum of Natural History, a few other things stood out. Mozambique's native language is Portuguese, a fact I had not known. Their money unit is the metical and during our visit, inflation raged, so $10 US dollars equaled $250,000 meticais. Paying for an item with dozens of heavy, wrinkled over-sized bills (many places didn't take credit cards), besides being confusing, felt unusually tactile, and definitely like I was handling play money.

Calculating a 500,000 MZN dinner tab

Also, we never bumped into another American, and even at the mesmerizing Natural History Museum—a must-see stopover full of taxidermied animals, exquisite handmade crafts, and rare, historic tribal artifacts—no other visitors appeared. What made the museum so unusual was that items were openly displayed, as if telling the public to "reach out and touch me." I feared these relics could easily be (and apparently have been) lifted from the unguarded building. But, the museum's most compelling sight was a stunning display of elephant fetuses, most preserved in formaldehyde; they ranged from one to eighteen months of gestation. That exhibit meant eighteen female elephants died in their prime.

On our way back to Johannesburg, through Swaziland, we'd driven a relatively short distance, when the Swazi countryside suddenly grew greener, lusher and hillier than any I'd seen thus far in Africa. Picturesque villages were dotted with round mud houses, all topped with thatched roofs. Houses flying white flags meant a marriageable young woman lived there; a red flag meant she was taken.

After touring the dry bush in Kruger, deforested Johannesburg, and war damaged streets in Maputo, Swaziland's verdant landscape looked like a gift from Mother Nature, who'd gussied up this route so visitors wouldn't leave Africa without seeing her dressier side. The scenery was further illuminated by Swazi women in bright colored skirts and head scarfs.

Much about Swaziland is centered on King Mswati III, an absolute monarch and polygamist. His father, the previous monarch had about 70 wives. Mswati III, at the time of our visit, was married to a dozen women, and according to Robert, had multiple concubines and a plethora of children.

Royal relatives are scattered around the country and the world. In Swaziland, they were identifiable by red feathers in their hair, such as the doorman at our hotel. Several years before, my mother had told me that a Swazi prince moved into the apartment next to hers.

My take was that the guy was trying to impress my mom. Now I believed he could easily be a Swazi prince.

After passing through Manzini, the city where King Mswati lived, we spent the night at the Royal Swazi Sun, another hotel designed with colonialism in mind. Incredibly, it was at this hotel where we met a couple from High Ridge, Missouri, a small town of 4000, about 25 miles SW of St. Louis. The two had been in Africa a month, and were headed to Maputo to scuba dive.

The next morning, November 28th, we made our way to the Mbabane, Swaziland "bus depot," an informal outdoor market marked by noise and haphazardly parked taxis, small trucks and "buses," known as Zola Budds. Such vehicles, named after the speedy South African Olympic runner, are the equivalent of a twelve seat van. Colin managed to latch onto a decent-looking bus/van going to his next destination, Durban, South Africa.

When I dropped Colin off, it felt more like an abandonment. Glancing back at him standing there with his rumpled outfit, lopsided dreads, and pitifully small backpack to carry him through nine more months of hard living, nearly broke my heart.

————

Robert and I immediately headed to Johannesburg, from where I'd fly home the next day. The highway was excellent, but virtually empty of traffic, and I worried about carjackers. South African crime was rampant, with carjackings being a leading offense on city streets and rural highways.

Earlier, at the Swazi hotel, something held me back—probably, Colin's next destination being Durban—from telling Robert or Colin about the conversation I overheard between two charter bus drivers, concerning a near ambush one of them avoided on the highway to Durbin. Part of their back and forth went like this:

"Hell no, I never thought of stopping. I didn't dare."

"Did you hit him?"

"No, he jumped out of the way just in time, but I would have hit him, because I wasn't going to stop."

————

After five days in Robert's company, I not only felt comfortable, but safe with him as an escort. For one thing, I thought of him as streetwise and tough, especially after he told us how vicious the fighting was during his stint in the Angola-Mozambique war, which South Africa eventually joined to help Mozambique. Plus, Robert sort of looked a like a thug.

He was also a national guide (as opposed to site guides, Louie and Lawrence), a status that allowed him to take tourists into all nine South African provinces and neighboring countries. He had a conversational knowledge of several African languages and seemed savvy about customs and rules, including how illegal business was conducted. Having grown up in South Africa, he'd despised Apartheid and was a rule breaker. He married a Chinese woman, but that relationship ended in divorce. When we met him, he was married to an American woman and maintained homes in Michigan and South Africa.

About two hours into our road trip, without seeing another soul which was almost as unnerving as having a car follow you, I finally asked Robert, "Do you carry a gun in the car?" "Nooo." he emphasized. "You don't want them to catch you with a gun in your vehicle, or on your person. If they stop you, you just give them what they want."

Aloe tree

Termite hill

■

Chapter 11

Back Home

December 3, 2003
To: Colin
From: Mom
Hi Colin,

Since I've been home, I've been rattling on nonstop about Africa. On reflection, Robert was greatly responsible for making it so memorable. He knows so much about South African history and present-day government. Also, he's very candid about his life, so I shared some of my concerns about your safety. He agreed that you must in all ways be careful. He mentioned more than once that AIDS is prevalent; said try not to stand out, keep your dreads tied back, and trust your gut.

That prompts me to say that when I met you in Cape Town, I felt something internal had shifted to lessen your interest and ambition in academics. Just a few months before, that had been your life force. I worry about you. You are precious to all of us. Even Brennan agrees you must take care.
Love,
Mom

From Durban, Colin insisted that he was polishing his grad school applications and deciphering FAFSA, EFC, SAR and other financial aid acronyms, while also deciding how and where he'd spend the next eight months of his trip. His self-imposed deadline for completing his essays had passed, but I didn't ask about them again. I hadn't forgotten months ago when Mike said, "Maybe Colin doesn't really want to get a PhD." I'd wanted Mike to be wrong, and still had high hopes for my son, who'd been passionate about teaching, and had been so successful with young people, especially troubled students. I felt he'd make an excellent professor, or academic, maybe at some think tank. Even Mike, before his pessimistic pronouncement, thought that with further study, Colin could try to get on staff at *The Economist* magazine; combine his interests in travel, writing and world affairs.

As Christmas approached, Colin wrote from Beline, Mozambique. He and a new friend, Greg, were planning to hitch back to Muputo, but he didn't explain why. At least he had a friend, but hitching was dangerous—drivers who robbed you, highwaymen like the bus drivers described, animal attacks, accidents....

———

It's funny how we change over the years. When I was a twenty year-old student in Bregenz, and planning a second long hitchhiking trip, this one during Christmas, robberies and car accidents never worried me. As a female, however, sexual predators were always a concern, especially after the creep I encountered the first time. But, one unpleasant incident couldn't dampen my enthusiasm. By then, the travel bug was so engrained in us, almost every student left at Christmas break, and scattered throughout Europe.

My destination was Spain, a country I figured to be as different from Austria as any in Europe. Also, after eight years of studying Spanish, I'd get to speak it. Daniel Remine, one of the guys in our group, also wanted to see Spain, so he and I planned to take the train to Italy, and then hitchhike from there. Because of the holiday, hundreds of young Italian workers were also heading to Genoa, our first stop. To avoid squeezing into a second class car with a bunch of rowdy men, we splurged on the first class overnight compartment. In Genoa, we caught a city bus, for 33 liras (about 33 cents) a piece, to the edge of town, then hitched a ride in a sporty convertible along the scenic Route de Corniche, passing right above Monaco, which Dan remembers being "lit up like a jewel." We made excellent time that first day, catching a last ride at sunset that dropped us on the outskirts of Nice.

That year, I was studying two new languages, German, a required class, that became my favorite subject, and French. In the spirit of studying foreign languages in foreign lands, I chose a new one, French 101 because I needed an elective. Unfortunately, that turned into a bloody nightmare, primarily due to my friend, Brian. Since Brian and I were the only students in the class, it was held inside our instructor's small cramped office at the hotel. That instructor, Madame Pinette, was also Dr. Pinette's very proper and elegant wife. As fate would have it, Peekie, Madame's adored toy poodle, who frequently farted, always sat on her lap during class. To Brian, those farts were like handing out *Playboy* magazines to a giggly thirteen-year-old, which was about where Brian's maturity level fell. Dan was quieter and more serious than Brian, and he didn't giggle. He also understood the advantages of pre-planning. Compared to the Autobahn/no sleeping in the airport/Amsterdam whorehouse caper with Brian, this three day, 850 Km (530 miles) jaunt to Spain was drama free.

However, at the hotel in Barcelona, I began hearing a woman in the next room plaintively repeating something in French. Fearing she might be in real trouble, I knocked on her door. "Come in," she urged, "I'm sick." The woman, an American named Elizabeth, was from Massachusetts. What she'd been repeating was *aidez-moi*, which sounded like a French word I should know, but didn't. Truthfully, because of Peekie and Brian, I was hardly learning anything in my French class. But, a*idez-moi* means "help me" and isn't too far off from *ayúdame*, "help me," in Spanish. Besides help, Elizabeth also wanted some ice cream. Lying there among a twisted heap of bed sheets, she looked way more sorry for herself, than sick. At any rate, the hotel brought up the ice cream, which revived her spirits, as did having a friendly English speaker next door.

I left Elizabeth to recuperate and joined Dan for a late Christmas Eve dinner. Later, we found a cathedral near a plaza, with a blazing bonfire reflecting smiling, rosy-cheeked revelers and worshippers. Among the crowd, and also far from home, were several US sailors, all of us preparing to attend midnight Mass. The Latin service had all the solemnity befitting the occasion—music, pomp and pageantry—rituals that Catholics do so well. I grew up Catholic, but Barcelona was the first time I attended Midnight Mass.

The ailing Elizabeth quickly recovered. When Dan talked to her the next day, he told her that he grew up in Massachusetts and attended high school in Swansea, a place Elizabeth knew intimately. She'd just had an affair with one of Dan's former high school teachers, who'd unceremoniously dumped her a few weeks before Christmas. In my mind, that had much to do with what ailed her.

An unexpected benefit to this Spanish trip was that Lisa Pappo, one of our Bregenz schoolmates, lived in Barcelona, where her father's international company transferred the family. On Christmas Day, Mr. Pappo graciously chauffeured us around Barcelona, pointing out the sights and then invited Dan and me to their home. The Pappo's were Jewish, but they hosted a memorable Christmas evening, topped with a festive holiday meal.

The next day, Dan said goodbye and set off to explore Spain on his own, while Lisa and I bought first class train tickets back to Bregenz. Even though I earned extra cash, I was running low on money. Student loans and a scholarship had financed the bulk of my education, but my mom also sacrificed to get me here. Unless it was an emergency, I wouldn't ask my mother to send money, especially not to gallivant around Europe.

This was the halfway mark of my year abroad. A few students, for varying reasons—financial, graduation requirements, unhappiness—now left the program and returned to Wagner or their home colleges. I remember thinking how glad I was that it wasn't me leaving. There's a scene in the movie, *American Graffiti*, when Steve (Ron Howard) decides to pass on going to college and remain in Modesto with his girlfriend, Laurie (Cindy Williams). That ending sets my heart aflutter; not because it's romantic, although in some ways it is. My heart wobbles because that could have been me skipping Bregenz because of a boy; a boy whose face, name, identity, has totally disappeared from memory. Instead of a life of regret, I spent a year discovering the unfamiliar, and becoming intoxicated with travel.

When I arrived in Austria, I deposited $500 in the bank to last me the year. It would be tight, but as a frugal person, I figured I'd live within the boundaries of Arthur Frommer's popular book, "Europe on $5 a Day," the go-to guide for thrifty travelers. My stay would last about nine months, and minus incidentals, like toiletries, all lodging and meals were prepaid, including school vacation trips. Often days went by, sometimes weeks, when I didn't spend a cent. There was a broad socio-economic cross section of students in our program, so I wasn't the only one who minded her money. In the 1960s, Wagner College was a conservative place with deep roots in the Lutheran Church. But this European program attracted a more diverse group than the home campus with a predominance of local kids from Jersey, Staten Island and Brooklyn.

In Bregenz, we had devout Christians, but also atheists, agnostics, free spirits, homosexuals, Daryl, an ex-pat whose father worked in Brussels, Suzanne, a well-traveled US Army officer's daughter stationed in Germany, and students from outdoorsy Northern and Midwestern states who already skied like Olympians and cared about the environment. Carol, from Hood College, had attended high school in Kabul, Afghanistan before the Taliban arrived. Americans were welcomed then, including her father, a Pan American airplane mechanic who trained Afghans in airplane maintenance. This wild, rugged country was still free of the Taliban but, like today, women were subjected to men's brutality—American media just didn't write about it. Carol described an incident when assailants burst into a school and cut every girl's face that wasn't covered in a burqa.

Lisa of Barcelona, by way of Canada, was our sole international student. I'd pegged her as "the rich kid," and I don't think I was alone in that assessment. But, after visiting her family, I didn't know how rich they were, but they certainly seemed comfortable enough that her train fare back to school would not be a luxury, as it would be for me.

Like me, most of the girls in our Bregenz group dressed like average American college students—in knee socks, skirts and sweaters. Nylons and heels were reserved for special occasions. I thought Lisa was rich because she swept through the hotel each day wearing nylons and heels. Many of us smoked then, but Lisa was the only one who walked around with a black cigarette holder, plus she wore a fur coat. Unlike my warm coat, with a rabbit fur collar, hers was full length fur, and Lisa had a habit of wearing it indoors, dramatically draping it around her shoulders, while looking like a million bucks with that cigarette holder.

The Weisses Kreuz Hotel

Chapter 12

The Teapot and the Tempest

Part of my tendency to over-worry situations with the kids was because their dad rarely worried about anything. Mike is the man who, on the night after Brennan turned twenty-one, yelled, "Well, goddamnit, leave his ass there," then rolled over and went back to sleep when we got a call from a police officer about 2:00 a.m., informing us that no one was hurt in a single car accident, but Brennan had rolled his car in a ditch and failed the DUI test. The court date would follow and if no one picked him up, he'd spend the night in lockup.

With my stomach roiling, and the worst pain hammering my head, I didn't know what to do, so I squeezed the pillow into my temples and lay back down to think. The designated driver concept was new and slower to penetrate college campuses, where Brennan now spent most of his time, and where students routinely walked home from bars. Often, Mike's refusal to stress out over the kids was the calming factor I needed, but it wasn't helping that night. Additionally, I was embarrassed that the cop heard what Mike said, and no doubt thought the worst of all of us.

I hadn't cared for one of the guys Brennan was with that night; a medical student with a nihilistic streak and a devil-may-care attitude. He was older, but hung around with a younger crowd. And he drank too much. A few years later, that troubled young man committed suicide.

Considering the seriousness of Brennan's offense, I concluded that Mike's tough love approach was probably best. Later, I also realized that what I'd seen was a father instinctively trying to mold a son into becoming a better man. It wouldn't have served Brennan well to come home and hear Mike say, "Go to bed, I'll talk to you in the morning." Much of the shock and fear would have worn off by then, but he'd never forget the humiliation of spending a night in jail.

Parents are advised to pick their battles. I fought daily skirmishes because Mike either didn't sweat the small stuff, didn't notice, had already left for work, or hadn't yet gotten home when something unacceptable took place, like Colin's tee-shirt morning. He was in 7th grade and bounded downstairs dressed for school in a black Bart Simpson tee-shirt that had a caricature of a black woman with blubber lips and huge buttocks that said, "Never Trust a Big Butt and a Smile."

Or, the "water balloon afternoon," when my boys, ages eleven and fourteen, were entertaining their seven year-old cousin, Houston, from Tacoma, Washington. A shy only child, Houston still had lovely manners and no experience with big brothers (or cousins) ganging up and playing dirty tricks. All three were mercifully outside, and Houston had finally forgotten about being homesick and was just running around, dodging most water balloons thrown his way, and only getting moderately wet—which was just the way he liked it. Sure enough, one of my kids, probably Brennan, the more expert dirty-trickster, came inside, went upstairs and, from the second floor window, dropped a fat water balloon on this sweet child's unsuspecting head.

Mothers and maybe all women recognize children's crying sounds that range from the fakey-wakey, to a cry of shock, followed by a three-second pause of disbelief as the pain builds. Then, a scream of unbearable torment erupts, like a tsunami washing over the injured body part—as when a car door once slammed on four small fingers. What I heard on my driveway was an unfamiliar, but deep guttural wail from the bottom of a grief-stricken little heart that had never felt so misused and dishonored in its entire seven years.

The list goes on and on, from me having to take a hammer to a misogynistic, vulgar rap music cassette tape; or the twelfth broken window—that last one in our house—and not, thank God, another basement or garage window belonging to Mr. Dwyer, Mr. Jones, Earl, Mr. Truman, Mrs. Eirten, or Mrs. Avery. By then, Mike had even taught them how to repair broken windows. Still, it was embarrassing to keep trying to arrange for your kid to get into a neighbor's garage or basement.

It's worth mentioning, that when Mike wasn't erupting over big and little boy screw-ups, he did his share of child care and spent more quality time with the boys than many men of his era. Even the messiest diaper didn't gross him out, although not much did, or does, unless Brussels sprouts count.

"No problem," he said, lavishly unrolling a roll of paper towels and joking about the poopy diaper in front of him. "I used to cleanup dog shit in our yard. This is a piece of cake." When the boys bathed together, they liked Mike to give the bath, because he didn't say, "Okay, enough; outta the tub," if they splashed water on the floor, or played a little too long with their toys. But their favorite hour together was bedtime, with their dad reading about Mike Mulligan's steam shovel, or them saying good night to the moon or hearing for the umpteenth time, how Alexander's, no good, very bad day went.

Mike's blowouts with the kids occurred infrequently, but they were usually duzzies, and it didn't matter that the offending son was three year-olds because, "Goddamnit, I just cleaned that basement. Put those two little fuckers on the phone," he bellowed through the line, "so I can ream them new assholes." I was standing in the kitchen with one month-old Colin on my hip; beside me were two wide-eyed toddlers, Brennan and his pal, Paulie, who heard Mike, got the picture, and was shaking his head, "No." They'd just come upstairs from our unfinished basement playroom, with grass seed in their hair. A quick check downstairs revealed that they'd first squirted Mike's oil gun around the floor, before confetti-ing it with seed.

Mike totally lost it over "the other car incident." The one that happened when Brennan was a sophomore in high school and we thought my car had been stolen. Mike and I returned home unexpectedly early that afternoon, pulled into the garage, and saw that my car wasn't there. We commiserated and ruminated, checked again inside our tiny two car garage, and still no car. "Did you drive somewhere," Mike asked, "then forgot you drove and walked home?"

"No, definitely not. I'm telling you, it must have been stolen. I'm sure I left it in the garage, but it doesn't look broken into, and the door was closed. Besides, it was there when we left. Wasn't it?" Finally, at a loss for what else to do, I called the police and we glumly sat on the front steps waiting for them. Instead of the police, fifteen year-old Brennan drove up in the car, with his buddy Andy in the passenger seat; twelve year-old Colin was sitting in back.

When Mike rushed the car, arms waving, Brennan backed out of the driveway and his dad took off after him, screaming, "Come back here you son of a bitch." Fortunately, Brennan had second thoughts about further driving, did a U-turn and unfortunately smashed into Mrs. Anderson's car.

Andy, no stranger to shit storms at our house—several inspired by him—bailed out and ran. I rushed inside and breathlessly called the police again, yelling, "Our car is back. Our son took it without permission and I'm afraid my husband might kill him! I've never seen him so mad"

"Ma'am, ma'am, does he own a weapon?" Thank God for small mercies. "Nooo," I wailed at the dispatcher, "we don't have guns in our house." I wanted to add, but didn't—Are you kidding? Look what they just did with the car!

The boys had taken a joy ride to East St. Louis, Illinois and were scared enough to confess that it was their second fling over there. Their punishment was a month of grounding, each. Additionally, Brennan couldn't get his drivers license for four more months, instead of two months, when he turned sixteen. I had been looking forward to sixteen, because living with a fifteen year-old was like waiting for a time bomb to go off. It was hard to fathom how a kid could be so smart in some ways, and dumb in others. At times, it seemed like Brennan had gone deaf, and misplaced his brains. "Up his ass," according to his father. Plus, there was a problem with punishment—they always took it like champs. With Brennan being the youngest kid in his class, everyone except him already had their license and he was happy catching rides with older kids.

After homework and dinner, Brennan experimented on the computer, and Colin gladly stayed upstairs reading *MAD* magazines or one of his boy-book series until midnight, if we let him. Colin didn't get in trouble as often as Brennan. A quick study, he kept his head down, learned from his brother's screw-ups, and generally knew which parental buttons not to push. Also, unlike his big, exuberant brother, whose gears I could almost see grinding up elaborate mischief—and thus often getting caught—Colin was a living maxim of see, speak and hear nada.

Cell phones weren't around yet, nor was there a phone, TV, or computer in their rooms. In a fit of fury, I'd already thrown the Nintendo set out the second floor window, but kids are wily critters who mess with your value system. About six months after I destroyed it, Colin earned enough babysitting money for a new Nintendo. No longer furious, and impressed by his ability to save, and finesse me, I let him buy a new one. Besides, I felt they'd learned a lesson and would stop sneaking downstairs to play in the middle of the night.

The day after the 1988 "stolen car" caper, I went to work looking for reassurance that Brennan wasn't turning into a car thief. Scott, my co-worker, often seemed to get a thrill by entertaining an office full of women with stories about death-defying, parent-infuriating stunts he and his three brothers pulled when they were kids. I told him what Brennan did and where the boys went.

"So," I asked him, "how did your parents react when you or one of your brothers took the car without permission?"

"Terry," he answered, with this funny look on his face, "we never did that."

"Oh, come on Scott, this is serious."

"No, shit. None of us ever did that. We'd be dead."

Oh God, I thought, these boys are killing me.

———

As for East St. Louis, it's a small river town about 10 miles away, and across the Mississippi River from downtown St. Louis, Missouri. Many of its 30,000 inhabitants are solid blue color and middle class citizens, but the city has long struggled with poverty and crime. Co-incidently, and shortly after the boys' venture, I had to visit a women's organization in East St. Louis for my work. The town's streets were laid out like your average city grid but, on block after block, everything had been razed, and most of the remaining dirt plots had been neatly plowed. Intermixed with these tidy baren tracts—that looked ready for planting—were a few tenement-type buildings.

After about eight or ten blocks, I hadn't seen another car or a pedestrian. I also found it odd that East St. Louis had no stop signs and none of the traffic lights were functioning. I just eased through them, hoping a cop didn't see me. Once at my destination, one of the first things I asked the receptionist who greeted me was, "Why didn't I see any working traffic lights or stop signs while driving here?"

"They've all been removed or disabled," she explained, "to cut down on carjackings, robberies and shootings."

Tribal artifacts in Mozambique History Museum

Chapter 13

Christmas on Two Continents

During the Christmas season of 2003, we weren't hearing much from Colin. Then, out of the blue, Colin's girlfriend, Aggalia, who was in St. Louis, called and with no preamble said, "Mrs. Mulligan, Colin needs you to wire him the $3000 in his savings account."

"Oh, dear God, please don't tell me he's been arrested and is sitting in some Mozambican dungeon! My worst nightmare! Does he need bail money? Is it to pay a bribe to get out of jail? Oh, my God, this is going to kill me. Do we need to find a lawyer to help him? Tell me, what's the money for?"

"I don't know," she said. "he didn't tell me."

"How could he ask you to make a call like this and not let us know what it's for? Why didn't he call us if he was in trouble? Oh, it's so frustrating not to be able to reach him or someone else over there to get some answers. Damnit, I don't even have a phone number for Robert!"

Finally, the next day, we got an email.

From: Colin
To: Mom
January 3, 2004

"mom, aggalia said you were worried about the money issue. it's just that greg, the guy i met in Beline, and i are going to partner for some wheels so it will be safer, easier and faster to get around.

a perfect example of why this is a good idea is that i ended up on the goat bus, from Maputo to Beline. a distance of about 190 kilometers took 14 hours, because every few miles we stopped at a village for a passenger, or passengers, who needed to tie their goats, bicycles, or jukebox-size burlap sacks on the roof. we left at 7 a.m. and got to Beline at 9:30 fucking p.m.

plus, there was also another bus ride, when I was at war with a sack of potatoes. They were under my seat, and after so many hours, the cockroaches cooped up inside had enough and started using my legs to escape. you would have been proud of me, that I didn't make a scene.

when you were here, you pointed out how unsafe the taxis are, so if you could wire me the money asap, i could get started on the next leg of this venture.
the reason I'm back in maputo is because we can get a good deal here. everything's fine, so stop worrying.
  love, c

January 7, 2004
To: Colin
From: Mom

I supposed we should be relieved to learn this is about a car and that you aren't in some underground prison, and I am. But this could have been handled without putting me through 24 hours of hell! Frankly, your dad and I feel that things have kind of stalled in Africa. Your plan was to see as much of the world as you could in a year. Mozambique is really cool and all, but maybe you could be doing a little more with your time than just playing on the beach.

We're wondering about a few things, like the car, which you seem to own, but haven't used much. Now that you need to go to Jo'burg, or whatever, you can't use it. It seems reasonable to have used it to take care of your ticket. Also, how do you and Greg plan to dissolve joint ownership? We really hope this was a sound investment. Technically, none of this is any of our business since it's your money, but for reasons we both know, I'm usually unavoidably involved in your plans while you are over there. Also, I value our close relationship and I think you'll respect my desire to speak honestly.

It's getting late, plus this message is a lot to read, digest and respond to-- and maybe you should take a little time to think all this over before you respond.
Love, Mom

———

During the next several weeks we emailed sparingly and Colin avoided mentioning the car. Instead, he wrote about his travel plans. Australia was on his bucket list, but he'd first need to have his discounted Student Travel Association ticket rewritten, and the nearest STA office was in Johannesburg. A short time later, he thought he'd be better off going to China. Aggalia, his girlfriend, had gotten a job teaching English in Shanghai, and he considered joining her on her two week spring break. Afterwards, he'd tour China on his own.

I too treaded lightly on my misgivings—which weren't only about the car. He was increasingly indecisive, graduate school now seemed iffy, and there was no plan B, or C. I had to be careful to not piss Colin off enough to stop keeping me informed. He was a self-supporting grown man, and generally savvy about handling money. Still, spending $3000 to own half a car in Mozambique seemed dubious, at best.

But, then came the double whammy on the car.

From: Colin
February 16, 2004
To: Theresa Mulligan
Subject: coming clean

hello—
ok, here goes: if you remember, i have never actually used the word "car" to describe my purchase (exact word was 'wheels'). i bought a small, new, mint condition motorbike in maputo, not a car. greg and i hitched back here to maputo to buy good bikes.

it's a 125 cc engine; the second smallest that is commercially available, and since the roads are

so filled with potholes, we spent most of our
time cruising at around 40 mph, until I became
comfortable and capable. i have a quality helmet
and safety rules--no riding at night, in the rain,
etc. the reason we stayed in maputo so long was
for the paperwork, but also so i could learn to ride
safely, change the tires, chain and oil, and basically
learn how the thing goes together and comes apart
before heading up north.

before you freak out about this, remember that
my only other option would be to take sheas—
minibus taxis like we rode in cape town—that are
often operated by profit-driven men who care little
about anything but putting moving cars on the
road. there are never seat belts. sometimes doors
are held on by coat hangers, and some don't even
have steering wheels--only vice grips plugged into
the steering column.

about 85% of accidents here are minibuses. these
guys seriously dont give a f--k. when comparing
the odds of getting there safely on one of those
things versus a bike that takes me slow but steady,
and is dependent upon my reactions and sense of
safety, the decision was easy.

i agonized over whether to tell you from the
beginning. like you, i value the closeness of our
relationship (and feel it has grown stronger since
you came to s. africa). i felt bad enough about
deliberately misleading you, but i would not tell you
a flat out lie--and that's the reason i've avoided
some of your questions.

i'm sure that you (and dad) are going to be pissed, but i PROMISE you that i've thought this through and it is a safe and memorable way to see the dark continent. most of my large cash expenditures were a one time thing: buying extra tires, tubes, chains, sprockets, etc. also, greg is such a good friend, who keeps reminding me to slow down and that it's foolhardy to begin a mission before the time was absolutely right.

plus, i gave a friend some money when he had nothing. he's a local dhow (sailboat operator) whose house burned, with every cent he had in the world. a few weeks before, his brother fell out of a coconut tree and died. he was truly desperate, not to mention crushed, and he didn't even have enough money to buy a bus ticket back home, so, no way i wasn't going to help him out--in spite of the financial difficulties it caused for me.

i felt that i should clear the air. so, there it is. i'm sorry for misleading you, and hope that you trust my judgement and forgive me. my silence was a desire to keep you from worrying until i knew how to ride safely—i've felt like a real rat for the past few weeks.

having said that, i guess i'm still a little confused as to why you think that i've lost my way here in africa. i feel that being here has taught me so much about humanity, and about the world which i hope to study, learn and teach about. i know it is a mother's job to worry (and criticize) but i promise you that i am better and healthier (physically, mentally and spiritually) than ever. ok, i guess that's enough for you to contemplate from one email.

love, c

———

Oh, God, a motorcycle! Whatever possessed him? After I got his email, I felt that from then on, Colin was in God's hands. In many ways, but mostly because he was still safe despite making questionable choices, I already felt God was looking out for my son. Additionally, I think my relatively calm reaction to the bike meant He was now also looking out for me.

The footloose nature of Colin's trip had been much harder on me than Brennan's. And, even though Brennan found community and kinship among likeminded diving enthusiasts, he saw his share of danger but, mercifully, I never heard about it until he returned—including him running out of air, during his first 20 meter dive.

Despite loving every part of my African trip, it probably didn't help that, while there, I'd heard too much talk about assaults, robberies and murders.

But really, a motorcycle! Neither of my boys had ever displayed a desire to own or ride a motorcycle because they knew the danger. Since the bike was already out of the garage, so to speak, I avoided even mentioning it in my emails. I also didn't comment on him helping the friend who, after his brother fell out of a coconut tree and died, had his house burn down with all his money inside. I knew Colin would get angry at my second-guessing him over such a "tragedy," and I'm sorry son, but it sounded like total BS. When he reads this now, some thirteen years later, he'll still get mad. But, on the flip side, any mother is grateful to have kindhearted kids (Brennan has reacted similarly to distress calls), whose first impulse is to help their fellow man.

————

After I absorbed this new reality, our correspondence switched to practical matters. Colin was offered a job as bookkeeper, including an apartment at a car dealership in Tofu. Because he loved the city, he'd think about it, although apparently not much. In that same email, he lamented dealing with forms, fees, and mountains of bureaucracy that held up his bike's official ownership document, so he could hit the road. Finally, when the document arrived, it freed him to head north towards Malawi, but he was sorry to be leaving Tofu and splitting up with Greg, his riding buddy of two months. Greg's allotted holiday was winding down and he needed to turn his "bony" around and head home to South Africa.

Colin's loaded bike

"Tofu," Colin wrote, "was the vacation within the vacation. I did little else but lay on the beach, party, smoke pot, ride my motorcycle and eat. I also had to go to [the city of] Maxixe to sort out my visa problems and negotiate my way out of a 16,000,000 Metacais fine." The Tofu beach parties were at a bar that had a dancehall, deck, welcoming camp fires, and cool Indian Ocean breezes. He'd also miss playing soccer on the beach with cute kids who came around selling candies, cashews and water, then stayed to have fun.

The most substantive part of these several email exchanges was, of course, the job offer, because it meant that someone thought he might be good for a role other than a motorcycle riding, backpacking, pot smoking, beach bum.

In late February, after almost two months in and out of the cities of Maputo, Beline, Xai-Xai, Chidinguele and Tofu—all in Mozambique—he geared up for his first solo trek to Malawi, which he expected would take ten days. His starting leg was a 375 Km ride to Vilankulo, then on to Inchope where he spent the night:

To: Mom
From: Colin
March 5, 2004
Re: Amerigo

i made it to within 10 kms of the malawi border, but had to stop for the night. i found a small house and asked the father of an extended family if i could camp in his yard. A skinny, toothless, grizzled old guy, he spoke almost no english, but we conversed well enough when he spoke slowly in portuguese. they thought my tent was really cool. anyway, they were dirt, dirt poor and had almost nothing, but

the father (amerigo) was very hospitable. he kept
helping with my tent, which probably extended the
time it took to put up by half--and making sure i
was comfortable. he even swept the dirt away from
where i wanted to pitch it.

i was exhausted and had no food, or water (just
iodine purification tablets), and was completely
filthy. we sat on his small porch (under an overhang
made of scrap wood), and they put up the mosquito
net. they had a small radio and i was up for hearing
mozambican music, one last time. in my honor,
he insisted on english, so i fell asleep listening to
evangelical sermons broadcasting from zimbabwe.

i went back to my tent around midnight and woke
up about 5 am, all ready to go, but i had a flat
tire—a small puncture had leaked all night. anyway,
it would have been a long, hard job by myself, but
i gave amerigo my last dollar bill and he sent some
kids to the store. they came back with some locally
made honey and fixed the tire in about a half an
hour. i traded addresses with amerigo and gave him
my only memento from st louis; my st louis rams
hat. he loved it and wore it until i left.

i crossed the border, and headed on to blantyre,
the second largest city in malawi. the road was
horrible and i averaged about 30 kms an hour. i fell
once in a deep patch of mud. no damage, but i was
covered once again in shit, to go with the still damp
shit from the night before. honestly, i don't even
want to think about how i smelled. the road then
varied between awful and excellent, and i made it

up into the mountains by four p.m., and cruised into town just before dark last night.

blantyre is a city of about 400,000 people; high in the mountains, and the drive in was amazing—sharp curves and long patches where you could look down into valleys on either side. it's the rainy season and there was a small rainstorm on either side of me, and i was cruising along watching the rain fall into the valley on either side of me, and it was fucking AMAZING!! it was sunny today, so i did the drive again. the view was clearer, but i think i liked it better yesterday.

March 7, 2004
To: Colin
From: Terry

I am so glad to hear you arrived safely!! Some interesting news: At a party last night, one of the women teaches at Wash U law school with another professor who is the brother of Malawi's President. She'll see if the St Louis brother is willing to set up an intro should you get a chance to call on the prez. After the security and paranoia around Mozambique's president, I don't know if such things are possible in Malawi, but it would be a highlight if you met him. Gotta run. Take care with mosquitos, water, traffic, the whole shebang.

I love you, Mom

March 8, 2004
From: Colin
To: Terry

now, it's just columbia's response. this is obviously
unexpected, and if i don't get accepted anywhere,
there are decisions to be made about next year—my
house, where i'd live, etc. staying in africa another
year and working over here is also an option. i
guess you were right about that ridiculous test
that was more important than i thought. news
about stanford ruined what up until now had been
a fantastic day.

you asked about racial discrimination over here.
it exists and a classic example occurred when I
was still in maputo and checking into fatima's, a
backpacking hostel. I was with greg, who's white and
amos, an african friend who works as a bartender. at
the hostel, the black security guard politely nodded
to greg and me. having not seen too many people who
look like me, they think I'm a dark skinned caucasian.
but the guard looked at amos with disgust. He's a
member of the Shangaan, a Tsonga-speaking ethnic
group who were among the first black laborers
recruited for work in south africa's gold and diamond
mines. Shangaan are known for hard work and
efficiency. a Zulu acquaintance told me the Shagaan
are often dismissed, by other tribes, as common
laborers who will do jobs 'prouder' tribes consider to
be beneath them.

in some ways the guard's reaction to amos reflects
the enduring success of the colonial regime's

strategy to divide and rule. their over-emphasis of minor ethnographic differences between local tribes established an artificial hierarchy, which in turn led africans to fight amongst each other, rather than focus on the true source of their oppression.
love, c

March 9, 2004
To: Colin
From: Mom
Re: Micro lending

Tell me more about your idea of studying micro-lending and how it helps your friend Duncan set up a telephone station. As for possibly staying in Africa another year, I think you should return home and get your head together. For six months, you've roamed like a gypsy. The changes in you were already apparent back in November. Three university doors have unexpectedly closed, and you don't want to give "the establishment" other reasons to do so again.

I worry about how disaffected one becomes with traditional procedures and standards after such a distant, unconventional trip. For instance, if you remain adamant or defensive about your appearance, it will definitely become an issue. There may come a time when dreadlocks are accepted in the professional world, but we're not there yet.

You mentioned that Aggalia talked to her school about you possibly teaching there in Shanghai. That could work, but without any prep time, you'll literally be coming in out of the desert and the bush to sit across from an educator who will judge you from a profession-al perspective. We can talk more about this, but please think about who, and what, and where you want to be in a year or two, or three.

I promise you, re-entry after a long absence in a foreign culture is hard. You will struggle to readjust when you get home. It happened to Brennan and to me when I returned from Bregenz. Both, Brennan and I were embedded in structured communities—daily routines, fellow students and town friends gave me a sense of purpose and be-longing. You, however, are winging it on your own, which can further distance you from a western perspective.

Everything in Bregenz was so clean, orderly and quiet. I got home in May, usually my favorite time of year. But, in shedding its winter coat, all of New York's ugly was magni-fied. I was depressed by the filthy streets, drivers laying on their horns, high decibel Boom Boxes, crowds. Additional-ly, old childhood friends were shipping off to Vietnam and might not survive. Overwhelmed and exhausted, I slept for what felt like weeks, before painfully facing responsi-bilities, like finding a summer job. I still had another year of college, which didn't excite me, but the thought of a school routine steadied me through the summer. On the flip side, I worried about what to do after college. I even-tually settled in, but Bregenz changed me, and not just by introducing me to distant lands. Some inner turmoil was due to becoming my own person. I still didn't know what I wanted to be, but now knew how I wanted my life to be—orderly. It helped some to become a neat freak: bed had to be made, clothes folded, no dishes left in the sink, no clutter. I still depended on Mom for sustenance, but if I could control my own space, life would eventually fall into place.

Brennan, like me, also had a home base in Dahab, with regular dive buddies and underwater goals, which provided structure and cushioned some re-entry shock. But, you were around that year and saw how out-of-sync he was—house-hopping, directionless, hesitant around old friends, confused by the economic downturn.

Gotta go. Much to do. More tomorrow, Mom

To: Terry
From: Colin
March 9, 2004

i have met dozens of people my age who came to work for agencies like care international, save the children, etc. seriously, mom, hardly any of them had a single good thing to say about their employers.

yesterday, duncan and another guy were telling me how much worse things have gotten in malawi since the advent of large-scale foreign aid programs. i am looking at microlending as a potential future dissertation topic, but if my research proves fruitful, it could turn into something significant. i completely agree that i need to spend some time getting ready for the applic. process, and preparing for the gre.
i'm still a bit puzzled by your aversion to me staying over here for a while longer. rejoining the establishment will take an adjustment, but

i will make it. i am also aware of the prejudices towards dreadlocks, however, it has been a while since you've seen me, and my admittedly shitty dreadlocks have finished growing. Ive been taking great care of them-and they look very respectable.

also, while staying at doogles—a hostel/bar/ restaurant—here in blantyre, I had an unfortunate encounter with a drunken malawi supreme court judge. He was riding his motorbike with his "niece" on the back. they plowed into my parked bike and trashed my fender. the judge's minion showed up next morning, asking me how to "make this right." all the local guys said I could really shake him down. the short version is that, by saying i just wanted enough to fix my bike, i came out ahead—5000 kwachas, about $50 US. it's a lot of money here—enough for repairs and any inconveniences.

i'm a bit under the weather today--sinus headache, slight fever and upset stomach--so i'm gonna wrap it up. i'll keep in touch about my plans, etc. happy thursday.

love,
C

From: Theresa Mulligan
To: Colin
March 15, 2001
Re: Amerigo and confused

That's a wonderful story about Amerigo. Really good that Duncan cautioned you away from digging into foreign aid and micro-lending. It stinks, but powerful and corrupt people could seriously take exception to you upsetting their gravy train. I wonder why officials can't change their procedures to eliminate the sleaze factor. Someone must be honest.

On a brighter note, on the 29th, I'm having lunch with Kim (Wash U law prof) and will tell her that you're still in Malawi (though barely). Her colleague seems to be dragging his feet on hooking you up with his brother. I'll see what's what with that. By the way, with possible job interviews coming up, are you planning on buying some new clothes?
Mom

Colin Mulligan:
Re: Hello
April 2, 2004
To: Theresa Mulligan

hi–

i am in mzuzu, malawi, about 300 km south of the tanzania border. i'm safe and sound, but sick. this is a good-sized city with places to eat, shop, rest and get better. my bike is in good shape but I have decided to sell it. On the way i camped two nights in cape mcclear, on lake malawi. its fortunes as a legendary lakeside resort have declined somewhat, partly due to the end of white-minority rule in neighboring rhodesia.

The quiet appealed to me and the first morning, i woke up to fishermen mending their nets on the beach, along with a few women doing laundry in knee-deep shallows. other than that, i was completely alone and at peace. The next day, my strength was fading as I made mad dashes to the latrine. i did nothing else except drink plenty of water, eat rice and fresh vegetables.

On Friday, I boarded the ilala, lake malawi's only passenger ferry. this legendary single hull steamer arrived from scotland in 1949 and was assembled here on the shore. it's a vital connection for remote villagers, and at each stop, they filled the lower deck with massive amounts of produce and, or livestock. after resting, i felt better and decided to get some exercise and swim to shore. there was no immigration office on the island so i didn't need my passport. plus, i thought it would be fun to dive off the top deck.

unfortunately, within an hour, the organism inside my gut sprang to life and, by the time we arrived in nkhata bay, my destination, i was weak as a kitten. the crew unloaded my bike, but i hired a kid who'd been panhandling on the pier to carry my heavy overladen backpack.

i booked a week at the hostel's campsite. an israeli woman was also there, trying to recover from malaria. i decided to see a doctor and headed to the only medical facility in the region. i hadn't weighed myself since durban. then I was a slothful 110 kilograms. now, after 10 weeks on the motorcycle, and 10 days of illness, i weighed 87 kilos. i'd lost 50 pounds.

a beautiful, young malawi woman entered, who was dressed in bright traditional clothing and held a tightly wrapped infant. when the doctor arrived, I motioned her to go ahead. she nodded her thanks and began peeling away her baby's blankets. what i briefly saw turned my stomach. his skin was covered with enormous lesions that leaked a foul-looking gelatinous discharge. it looked like shit flowing out of his skin. I still think about that boy and wonder if the doc helped him. unfortunately, the doctor did not fill me with much confidence about his curative powers. he looked at, not examined, me for five minutes, asked a few questions regarding my stomach and bodily functions, then gave me pills for stomach worms [i threw them away].

ironically, that week was among my most serene in africa. i lived a quiet simple life. cooking, washing, fetching water was done only from immediate need. no frills, no indulgence; just me living in the moment. the bike is good, but it's too expensive to keep and it'll fetch a fine price in dar es salaam. anyway, i'll rest here in mzuzu for a few and then i'm on my way to tanzania. you should expect the next message in about a week.

From: Colin Mulligan
To: Theresa Mulligan
Re: safe and sound in the haven of peace...aka, dar
es salaam, tanzania
Apr 8, 2004

"hi—
i came a good ways, and arrived a bit worn down
and sick. a few days ago, I put the bike on an
overnight train and crossed into tanzania. dar
es salaam is very exotic; african, middle eastern
with a touch of india. a great mix of music and
international food scene. very cool. anyway, i have
begun trying to sell the bike, and already have a
few interested customers. a number of NGO's I met
were interested, but they all wanted a new bike. i
hired a local travel agent to help me advertise it
at 7% commission, if they sell it. i doubt that i'll
get as much as i was hoping, but enough for an
enhanced airline ticket if i go to australia on may 3.

i've checked into a small hotel, the safari inn
limited, in dar es salaam. there's a phone in my
room, tel: 255-22-213xxx. I'll devote myself to
selling the bike before looking for plane tickets. has
columbia sent any word on admission?

Today was for organizational chores, so tomorrow
will be a tourist-type day. aside from that,
everything is cool. i'll look forward to hearing from
you soon. love,
C

To: Mom
 On Apr 9, 2004, Colin Mulligan wrote:

hi–
i think it's best to head to nairobi and use the
sta office there to redo my ticket, so I can get to
australia. the package i mailed will be souvenirs
that i traded for my old clothes--my riding gear
especially. it's easy to trade clothes for souvenirs,
then i'll get some nice new clothes for my change
of continents.

a filipino guy likes the bike. no one else beat his
600,000 tanz. shillings offer—about $575. It kills
me that the strong US dollar takes a bite out of
my ass. but the bike has helped me learn a lot of
lessons, one of which is that everything—including
lessons—has its price.

ok, thats about it. feel free to call again if you
want. it was good to talk to you guys last night.
love, c

———

During the last two weeks of April, Colin traveled by bus to Nairobi and reported getting very sore from walking around the city, after having ridden his bike for so long. The Nairobi STA office arranged a $227 flight to Shanghai, with a stop in Dubai. The Chinese embassy also issued a visa for China, but his plane didn't leave for five days and he didn't want to stay in Nairobi because it was "dirty, expensive and boring."

He spent five days outside of Nairobi at Lake Naivasha, near Elsamere, the game reserve made famous by the book, *Born Free*.

During colonial days, Lake Naivasha Country Club was used as an airport for British Airways seaplane service to East Africa; Colin described Naivasha as still the poshest spot around.

He wrote that each night, at his protected campsite, he heard hippos, elephants and other animals grazing, groaning and wheezing right outside his tent. When another camper from Swaziland offered to lead him on a walking tour at a much cheaper price than the regular guides; Colin took him up on his offer and they did their own night walk through a nearby private reserve.

> "i walked among dozens of giraffes, zebras and antelope. I also saw where a leopard had hidden his kill in a tree. lake naivasha is one of east africa's great bird watching spots, and i lost track of all that i saw—flamingoes, cranes, storks, doves, eagles. at my campsite every morning i awoke to a symphony of bird calls. very nice indeed."

While in Kruger Park, Colin and I had learned that these animal sanctuaries were good for thrills; the dangers were less apparent, unless they jumped out and grabbed you. Had Colin been listening when our Kruger guide described the stealthy nature of leopards? A wily leopard would stalk, then attack, with or without provocation, and who knows what it might have done if it caught interlopers around its unfinished meal.

At Kruger Park, a couple staying at our hotel went on a private evening walking tour, with a professional guide, and I remember two things about their departure. First, the woman was about as tall as Elmer Fudd and as goofy-looking in her spanking new safari outfit that was way too large for her elfin little body. Secondly, their guide had the biggest rifle, with the longest, thickest barrel I'd ever seen.

Kish Island

Chapter 14

The Middle East

Colin's first Middle East stop was al Ain, in the United Arab Emirates, a city bordering Oman, which he visited daily to use an Internet cafe. Despite the exotic pull of the Middle East, Colin didn't care for the UAE. He said it was boring and dirty, and also reeked of oil. On the upside, everything was inexpensive, except hotel rooms, which rented for $30 a night.

To avoid high hotel fees, he found a campground in Dubai and spent five, unexciting, and likely very hot days in a tent. His financial situation in St. Louis had shifted from secure to shaky. When the spring semester ended, the five students who'd rented his house moved on, thus ending the revenue stream that paid for his trip. So, a good idea, I reasoned, to forego $30 hotel fees and live in his tent, despite the heat.

Upon reflection, spending five days in the Arabian Desert, instead of moving on, seemed like an odd choice, but I still didn't have a clue, even after Brennan asked me, "Did Colin tell you where he was?"

"No," I answered, " but, he updated me today and he sounds fine."

I'd forgotten about that exchange with Brennan until about two years ago, when I started rereading these emails. Where Colin had gone thirteen years ago didn't matter much anymore, but re-reading it peeked my curiosity, so I asked Brennan if he remembered mentioning it. He did.

"So? Where did your brother go?" I asked.

"Iran."

"Oh God... I am really glad I didn't know that. When you guys were younger, I swear you were trying to kill me."

"Calm down. He only went to Kish."

"Kish? What is Kish? What are you talking about?"

"Look it up. That's what you used to tell us to do."

I fully intended to look it up, but first I called Colin. And, indeed, Kish, this place I never heard of was in Iran, the country that, in 2002, President George Bush had labeled—along with Iraq and North Korea—the Axis of Evil. I asked Colin why he went there.

"Why not? It's one place in Iran where you don't need a visa, so I took a 20 minute puddle jumper over from Dubai."

"Were you nervous? Did they search you when you arrived?"

"At the Kish airport, the only tense moment was when the immigration officer took me into an office. I didn't have any money and couldn't use my credit card, due to American sanctions. But the guy never searched me. He was really cool. He even wanted to share his dinner with me, because he felt bad about deporting me on an empty stomach. I'll tell you where they searched me—in Dubai. I was dressed in African clothes; I had the dreads, and they acted like I was a fucking Nazi."

"So, how did you get to stay in Iran?"

"Like I said, they were cool. They seemed to like me and wanted to help. They contacted some kind of money man who sets up short term accounts for tourists, so they can use credit cards.

Iranians didn't like the American government, or George Bush, but they were friendly and curious about Americans, and basically hated all the religious bullshit they had to deal with.

"Kish was once a fancy resort, but when I was there, everything was dirty and run down because the government didn't have any money. The island still had nice malls, hotels and beaches, but everything was frayed and needed cleaning and repairs. I stayed at a hotel for $30 a night."

On my own, I learned that Kish is an island located just off the southern coast of Iran in the Strait of Hormuz. Kish has two unique characteristics that differ from mainland Iran. It's a duty-free zone, so Iranians and tourists from around the world go there for the shopping. Also, the harsh rules and regulations that apply to the rest of Iran are more relaxed in Kish.

———

Over the next few days, with his money running low, Colin wrote that his best move was to get to Shanghai for an interview with a Mr. Zhu, that Aggalia, his girlfriend had arranged regarding a teaching position. We also told him about a family friend, Mr. S, an executive at an American company who regularly flew to Shanghai on business. Though doubtful, Mr. S was another possible contact for employment. Australia was no longer on his to-do list.

To: Terry
From: Colin
May 5, 2004
okay, about the mr. s thing. i haven't even thought
about my presentability for an interview, let alone
what i'd be qualified to do. i have nice looking
clean clothes—lots of african-looking stuff—but no

business attire. I am (cautiously) keen on the idea of working in Shanghai—after i get a chance to tour asia for a bit, though. a while back you were much more pleasant to write back and forth with. you actually sounded like you had confidence in me and what i was doing on the road....
if you'd continue to have some faith in me, and stop being so negative all the time, you might see that this is the opportunity that i've been waiting for all my life. this trip is not about "fun" or "partying," as you have frequently insinuated. most of the time, i am by myself; looking, listening, meeting people and contemplating all that's happened—that's why i took the opportunity to come to the middle east, even though it's hotter than a snake's ass here.
i miss you, too.
love, c

■

Chapter 15

The Far East

When Colin arrived in Shanghai, his girlfriend still had a few weeks before her spring break. At night, he hung out with her and her friends, but used the daylight to explore Shanghai and visit areas like the Bund, an historic waterfront business district that is often compared to old Wall Street, in New York City. The Bund is also the neighborhood where many of Shanghai's expats lived. His most memorable observation was:

> "Shanghai doesn't seem to have a sense of itself. 5000 years ago, Chinese civilization was at its peak for architecture, art and culture. Today, it's pockmarked with construction cranes that are modernizing an ancient city at a frenzied pace. When you eat at a good restaurant the waiter gives you an extra chair so your parcels won't get wet because of all the spit on the floor."

Other than finding tasty, unwatered-down wine, and observing Shanghai's transformation, not much went right. The school hadn't decided on hiring him, and he and Aggalia broke up, which might have been his first taste of the real world. He interviewed at a posh private school, in a sophisticated city, while wearing sneakers, and a mix of African garb, and hastily-purchased American knockoffs. Since he'd long ago chucked nonessentials—like deodorant—Aggalia's former honey bear, probably smelled more like a panda bear. Consequently, Colin felt the next best thing to do was head to Chengdu, China, which was on the route to Tibet.

> To: Colin
> From: Mom
> June 30, 2004
>
> Hi,
>   The whole tenor of your message unsettled me. One of the more troubling comments was, "I am almost ready to quit." What do you mean?? Quit what? That implies failure. How can you fail when your goal was to enjoy yourself, while seeing as much as you could in a year's time? If it's not fun anymore, come home. That's not quitting; that's being practical. You've passed enough tests and don't have to prove anything.
>   Frankly, the hard part might be in coming home, and maybe that's what you're afraid of. You might be wondering how to reconcile who you were, with who you are now. I don't think another three months of hard, lonely living will help you magically pull all those conflicting emotions together, while also worrying about what to do with the rest of your life. I was concerned before you even landed in Shanghai, and relieved that you "got off the road." Maybe you need to come in out of the cold (sorry for all the clichés, but they sort of work) and take it one day at a time.
>
> Love, mom

To: Mom
From: Colin
June 30, 2004
Hi,
i understand what you are trying to say, but i don't
think i made myself clear. when i say 'give up,' i
mean come home; nothing more or less. by giving
up, i mean coming home before i accomplished what
i needed to accomplish. the purpose of my trip is
not enjoyment. i'm in search of something very real
and my recent experiences have helped me learn
what that is. my thinking is very much inline with
dad's. getting shat on by grad schools may yet turn
out to be the best thing that ever happened to
me... i was a bit floored to read that you and dad,
who i have always regarded as quite grounded and,
well, close-minded, speaking of destiny...

my destiny—or at least a major stepping stone on
that path— is hidden here in asia, waiting to be
uncovered by exploration, learning, enthusiasm and
above all, belief that everything will work out in
the end. i will not come home now, but you should
take comfort in that i feel i only have one more
adventure to make before i return. i promise it
won't be long. i'm not crazy, and i'm not going to do
anything stupid. everything is okay. as i told you
in the email, i was feeling a bit overwhelmed and
alone yesterday and I needed to let it out. i'll be
leaving for chengdu tomorrow night. maybe i'll try
and call.

———

After a 40 hour train trip, Colin arrived in Chengdu, China, then flew to Lhasa, Tibet. He hooked up with two other Americans and an Aussie who spoke excellent Chinese. Their hotel was near the Jokhang Temple, the spiritual home of Tibetan Buddhism, and near the Dalai Lama's palace, the Potala. With the 10,000 foot elevation, he took it easy, spending hours sitting in the main square of the temple.

"the atmosphere there was unlike anything i had seen before. there were weathered old pilgrims walking around, doing endless sets of prostrations in front of the temple with the hope of winning a favorable rebirth; monks in scarlet and gold robes and filthy street children happily doing handstands and cartwheels to the delight of camera toting westerners.

"i was particularly struck but the "ethnic look" of the tibetans; it's like a cross between native americans and chinese with a touch of indian. they have such beautiful traditional clothing and jewelry, really something. There is such an air of nobility and gentleness about them that one can't help but be moved by their misfortunes. yes, quite a first day. more later."
love, c

Tibetan
mother and child

To Mom
From: Colin
July 11, 2004

hey mom—
Lhasa kicks ass. no other way to put it. i'm staying
in a comfortable dorm room for about $2.50 a
night; food is cheap and the place is mind blowing.
today i took a three hour trek up into the
mountains to a cave complex that's among tibetan
buddhism's most holy sites. guru rinpoche, the indian
sage credited with bringing Buddhism here, spent
seven years meditating there.

i hiked through the most amazing scenery—valleys,
snowcapped peaks and all. after hitching a ride on
the back of some dude's motorbike and taking a
cab through some of the worst roads ever, i finally
got there by hiking up with three monks from the
local monastery. we passed tibetan pilgrims, donkey
caravans and more mountain streams then I could
count. there were small "towns" and work areas
along the way, and every time we passed a group
of tibetans, they were all friendly smiles and hellos.
I've never met a nationality of people who are so
spiritual, welcoming and friendly.

the shrine, and impromptu temple, is overseen by
several local monks who graciously showed me
around. prayer rugs were tied up and down the
mountain in such volume that they looked like
red, white, blue and yellow spider webs. it was
beyond cool. i feel as though my whole trip has

been building towards tibet, i feel that once i see what I came to see here, i can come home with contentment and completion. please save the emails i've sent you. i've been making an honest effort to write about all the important stuff, and i'd love to read all of them when i get back.
love, c

———

While exploring the Himalayas, Colin swam in the sacred, but frigid turquoise-colored Lake Namtso, while surrounded by wandering nomads, migrating yak herds and spectacular scenery. The morning afterward, he awoke to a 40 degree temperature drop, with snow and ice on the ground.

Prayer rugs

He obtained a visa to Nepal, bought a warm coat, a North Face knockoff, and a $13.00 camera—finally—then took a 250 Km, eleven hour bus ride along the monsoon-muddied road to Shigatse. In

Shigatse, arrangements were made to get to Kathmandu, where he spent one night at a "pretty nice" $6 hotel, but planned on switching to cheaper accommodations. On July 23rd, Colin reached Mount Everest base camp (17,600 feet) and camped for four days, along with taking an 8.5 hour trek up to Camp 2. To travel from Camp 2 to Zhangmu, the border town between Nepal and China, he said, "i… hitched a ride with very nice Italian guys, in an expedition supply truck, who saw the condition of my feet and took pity on me." When they picked Colin up, he was wearing sandals, because his waterproof sneakers had gotten soaked and given him blisters. At that point, he was below the snow line, and temperatures had risen sharply, but ice melt running down the mountain swamped the road and the tops of his shoes, soaking them.

The truck let Colin off about 3 kilometers before the border, because they only had a permit for their crew. On his way down, he described the views as, "going from snowy mountains to a valley straight out of "romancing the stone," along with the sights, sounds and smells of the subcontinent. once in zhangmu i got my first look in the mirror (and first shower), in about ten days. needless to say, it wasn't pretty. now, here i am in kathmandu, enjoying the warm curry-filled and oxygen-rich air."

———

On August 4th, Colin flew from Kathmandu to Bangkok. At the STA office, he learned he had enough points remaining on his ticket to fly from Bangkok to Chicago for $70, but not until September 1st. When I heard from him on August 12th, he was in Pai—a small Thai mountain town, near the Burmese border—but promised he'd get back to Bangkok 3 ½ days before his flight home:

"the last few days have been totally kick-ass—trekking, elephant riding, bamboo rafting, motorbiking. by the way, i was just offered the job teaching in shanghai. i'll do some thinking over the next few days, but i'm about 99% sure that i'll say no. anyway, that's the juice for now."

From: Colin
August 19, 2004
Re: Laos
hi,
here in laos, i kind of fell ass-backwards into the 'right place.' tibet was very spiritual, but somewhat overwhelmed with rigid buddhist doctrine; laos is also very spiritual, but the beliefs are rooted in ancient pre-buddhist chinese philosophy, more in tune with forces of nature and the spirit world.

when the french colonized indochina, they characterized the three occupied nations by saying: 'the vietnamese plant the rice, the cambodians watch it grow, the laotians listen to it grow.' this will be my last email for a while, as i'm headed into the more remote northern parts of laos. i'm interested in meeting some of the hill tribes.

———

That was our final email correspondence. Colin called a few times before arriving home on September 2, 2004, backpack over his shoulder, like he always held it. He was thinner; he was still my Colin, but he wasn't the same person who left one year, two weeks and a day ago. His dreadlocks were longer, they were still a mess, but before he was done, his dreads would grow ten more inches.

After spending a half year among people living in abject poverty, Colin's world view shifted. Material goods were of no interest to him. Going green and being organic became his new priorities, including meticulously tending his yard, starting a backyard compost pile, and an aloe hair product business. "Mom," he said, at one point, "all you need in life is a roof over your head and clean water." Job after job turned him down and I began to suspect prospective employers weren't just seeing dreadlocks, but some dichotomy within this qualified, personable and once imminently employable young man.

To handle his duality and disappointments, Colin smoked a lot of pot—which he assured me wasn't habit forming. His dad talked to him; I talked to him, but we only heard, "Everything's fine." In August of 2006, this tailspin finally ended, when he interviewed for an adjunct opening in the Writing Center where I taught, and got the job. The Internet, and online documentation had taken off, and with his recent MA studies, Colin was ahead of the game. He mentored students, but also the staff, becoming the go-to guy for documenting everything from digital Bibles to YouTube videos. Later, he successfully petitioned the History Department Chair to teach a cornerstone class, The Geography of War. The better things went, the more renewed he felt, and the more ambitious.

Finally, Colin decided that living in New York would be better for him, and left in 2007. He stayed two weeks with my friend Jackie, who coached him on life in New York, including, how to navigate the subways. Next, he briefly rented a room with a gay, high-strung, bossy, disabled man with whom Colin got along, until he didn't.

Within weeks be found a job at a private high school, and an affordable apartment. Two years later, he met Masha, and in 2012, they married, and moved to Los Angeles, where he models and makes television commercials. It was only after a few dates with Masha that he cut his dreads and shaved his head. Today, he too travels whenever he can and recently, while in England, saw Greg, his motorcycle-riding buddy, for the first time since 2004.

Afterword

In 2001 and 2003, when my sons, with bulging backpacks and vague plans left to explore the world, they were in their twenties; old enough to know a few things, but wise enough to go with humility and open hearts. Thus, the great adventure found Brennan at 20 meters beneath the sea, when natural wonders like see-through glass fish helped him fall in love with scuba diving. Later, on his first advanced dive, along with adventure, Brennan was also granted beneficence, because he ran out of air, but surfaced safely, while sharing another diver's air tank.

Colin met adventure and grace on a Malawi mountainside, when he rode through his first sun shower with a rainbow hovering overhead. In Tibet, he hiked down a 15,000 foot mountain, and witnessed how "Tibet's unique climate and geography help balance the planet's ecosystem. Droplets of snowmelt trickled down the mountain, and met multiple streams that morphed into rapids. At the valley's bottom, those rapids became a churning river and a primary source of water for much of Asia."

My sons took risks; followed strangers into their homes, rode 44,000 kilometers alone into the heart of darkness, and camped with party-boy Bedouins. The rewards? Freshly cooked meals in family settings, sunrises viewed from venerated sites, beach soccer with little kids in Mozambique, and dominos with Bedouin bracelet girls, who cheated and called Brennan Boo (Boogeyman in Arabic), because he wouldn't let them win. Later, my guys kicked back with warm beer and Universalist friends while watching orange eventide ease beneath the sea. Young and old, rich and poor blessed them with kindness; others took them for fools. They ran out of food, got sick, lonely and sometimes despaired, but were also comforted by the divine nature of spirituality and mysticism. In the end, they found beauty in the world and in themselves.

While seeing them off, I prayed that all their adolescent screwups were behind them, but, if they weren't still risk-takers, they wouldn't have wanted to freewheel around Third World countries in the first place. When I look back now, I'm happy about my sons' travels which, like my year in Europe, continue to have benefits today. The world was viewed through a different prism when I traveled, but, some things remain static, like young people's dreams. I kept their emails out of fear that I might never see my boys again. During their absences, I tried to control my misgivings, but some itineraries and choices they made left me anxious for weeks.

While re-reading our correspondence, I realized how blessed I was that both boys regularly kept me informed. They lessened my worries, but I think home was also a reminder that they'd already traveled the easy road, and now needed to traverse new boundaries and test the unknown.

Acknowledgments

Thank you to Mike, my husband and toughest critic; and to Rick Skwiot for his suggestions and ongoing expertise. My Bregenz friends, Suzanne O'Keefe, Carol Lenza, and especially Daniel Remine, shared memories, photos and pointed out inaccuracies. Thanks to Judy Deutsch, Mary LaBarge, Kathi Crane, Phyllis Bernstein, Juanita Jahn, Colette Walsh, Lynn Giardina, Diana Drisko, CeCe Luecking, Joan Gerard, Ellen Usher, Peggy and Jim Crowe, Pam Wilson and Patty Giesler for reading parts or all of the manuscript. I owe a lot to Prateep Bandharangshi for putting my mind at ease by being Brennan's travel companion and for sharing his photos with me. And finally, thank you to Brennan and Colin for being adventurous, independent, and audacious enough to take these trips—and return home safely.

About the Author

Terry Baker Mulligan is the author of *Sugar Hill: Where the Sun Rose Over Harlem*, which won the 2012 IPPY Award for Adult Multicultural Nonfiction and two 2013 Benjamin Franklin Awards for Multicultural Writing and Autobiography/Memoir Writing. Her novel and second book, *Afterlife in Harlem*, was published in October 2014. Terry was born and raised in Harlem, and, like her sons, has traveled extensively on five continents. She now lives in St. Louis, where she was named one of the city's Top Fifty Authors by a government committee.